Me

T

THE MESSAGE

THE MESSAGE

Colin Fry

WINDSOR
PARAGON

First published 2009
by Rider
This Large Print edition published 2013
by AudioGO Ltd
by arrangement with
Ebury Publishing

Hardcover   ISBN: 978 1 4713 5709 1
Softcover   ISBN: 978 1 4713 5710 7

British Library Cataloguing in Publication Data available

Printed and bound in Great Britain by
TJ International Limited

I dedicate this book, as always, to my partner Mikey who is such a source of inspiration to me.

To my nephew Ryan—who I hope will always strive to be someone special.

To the memory of my grandfather Lawrence Briggs, who left this world many years ago, but who has never left me, and to my grandmother Freda Fry, who lived so long and so well.

The sand of the sea, the drops of rain, and the days of eternity—who can count them?

Apocrypha, Ecclesiasticus

CONTENTS

PROLOGUE

The Message

I am fortunate to have been born with the ability to receive and pass on messages from the spirit world. As you will discover as you read this book, we are all closer to that world than we can imagine. And we all have the ability to connect and feel their presence, to receive messages of our own.

During the course of my three decades as a medium I have been able to put thousands of people in contact with loved ones who have passed over to the other side. If I was asked to choose the most significant message I have received during that time, however, I would have no hesitation in choosing the one that was delivered to me when I was a ten-year-old boy. It changed the course of my life. Without it I might never have become a medium in the first place. Without it this book may never have been written.

It wasn't the first time that I'd communicated with the spirit world. Far from it. I have a feeling my life had been leading up to that moment since I was very young.

According to my mother, my ability to connect with the other side had been apparent since I was a baby in my cot. She once told me a story about how, when I was only a few months old, she had walked into the bedroom to check on me one evening. In the beam of the night light she had seen me giggling away at a baby's rattle suspended in mid air above the cot.

1

I have no memory of that. However, I do remember the moment, four years later, when I first got an inkling that I was able to sense things that other people couldn't.

A friend had come round to visit my mum at our home in Sussex. I had never met the lady before but it was clear to me that she and my mum must have been very close for a long time, since before I was born.

I was brought up in that generation where, when your parents had visitors, children were expected to be seen and not heard. You were expected to play quietly while your parents were entertaining. So while the lady was in the house I did what all well-behaved four-year-olds did: I politely said hello then kept out of the way.

It was only when the lady had gone that I asked my mother about something that had been bothering me during the visit. 'Mum, why was that lady ignoring the little boy with her?' I wondered.

My mother looked at me, slightly mystified. 'What are you talking about? She didn't have a little boy with her,' she said.

'Yes, she did,' I replied. 'The little boy who kept tugging at her coat.'

'What did he look like?'

'He had really, really curly ginger hair.'

'Don't be silly.'

'He did. And his name was John.'

She stopped and looked at me with a surprised expression for a moment then shook her head. 'You can't have seen a little boy.'

I knew what I had seen and wasn't going to give in. 'I did see him,' I insisted. 'He was with this lady and she wasn't listening to him.'

2

My mother had a box of family photographs that she kept on top of a cupboard in the living room. Rather than arguing with me any more, she got it down and started rummaging through the photos. 'Do you mean this little boy?' she said, pulling out an old black and white image. It was a fading photograph of a curly-haired young child, no more than four or five years old.

'Yes, that's him, John.'

'Darling, you can't possibly have seen him,' my mum said.

'Why not?' I asked, confused.

'Because he died five years before you were born.'

From then on, both my mother and I understood that I had an ability to see things other people couldn't. And we both understood that it was an ability that I had to use responsibly and discreetly. 'You can always tell me, but sometimes it's best not to tell other people you can see someone they can't,' she told me.

My mother never made too much of my ability. She never dismissed it. But she never made a fuss of it. Her attitude was that if it developed into something then it would develop into something. If it went away, it went away.

But, of course, it didn't go away, quite the opposite in fact. I had many other experiences during my childhood. I often saw spirit children, for instance. But it was when I was ten that I went through the most powerful and life-changing spiritual encounter of all.

It happened late one night when my brother and I were staying with one set of our grandparents, my dad's mother and father, a few miles away from

3

our home in Sussex. Our parents were at Guy's Hospital up in London, at the bedside of my maternal grandfather, Lawrie, who was gravely ill with cancer.

I was very close to my grandad Lawrie. He was a very quiet and shy man. He was blind in one eye and hunch-backed, and had spent his life working as a kitchen porter. Even though he did a simple job he was a highly intelligent man. He just wasn't hugely ambitious. Even as a child, however, I knew that still waters ran deep.

My grandad was a kind and gentle man, but what I particularly liked about him was that he talked to me like an adult. He always used to refer to me as 'Sonny Boy'. I always felt we had a special bond.

So I'd been very distressed by his illness. I'd been to see him while he was at a hospital in nearby Brighton and had been disturbed at how pale he looked. 'Why is Grandad so white?' I remember asking.

Since then, however, his condition had deteriorated and he'd been moved to Guy's in London, where they specialised in treating terminally ill cancer patients. My mother and father had been called up to London to see him that night and had dropped us off with my other grandparents. They hadn't told us how grave the situation was, although my mother's rather sombre mood as she waved goodbye from the car should have told its own story.

Looking back, I think it must have been 11.30 to 11.45 p.m. when I woke up suddenly. I was sharing the large bed in the spare room with my brother, who was still sound asleep next to me.

4

As my eyes adjusted to the dim light I saw my grandad Lawrie. He was standing at the foot of the bed and was wearing a shirt and a cardigan and a pair of trousers. I was really pleased to see him, not least because he looked well. The awful whiteness I had seen when I'd last visited him in hospital had left his face.

'Oh Grandad, you're out of hospital,' I said.

'Yes, I'm out of hospital,' he replied quietly.

'Are you better now?'

'Yes, I'm much better now. I am not going to be sick any more.'

As we chatted, my brother remained asleep, oblivious to what was happening.

As a young boy, I didn't really know that much about cancer. At this point I think I really believed my parents had brought Grandad home and that he really had made some kind of miraculous recovery. Why wouldn't I have thought that way? He was sitting there, chatting to me, after all.

'Where're Mummy and Daddy?' I asked.

'Oh, they'll probably be along later,' he said.

'So why are you here?'

'I've sort of come to say goodbye.'

'Goodbye?' I said, slightly confused now. 'Won't I see you again, then?'

He smiled. 'Oh yes, you'll see me again, Sonny Boy,' he said. 'But nobody else will.'

And then he faded away in front of me.

I was wide awake now so I went downstairs and found my other grandparents were still up. It must have been close to midnight. When I appeared at the foot of the stairs dressed in my pyjamas, my grandmother gave me a concerned look.

'What's the matter, darling?' she asked. 'Can't

5

sleep?'

'No, I'm fine,' I said. 'I just came down to tell you that Grandad Lawrie came to say goodbye.'

They just looked at one another, the shock etched on their faces. 'Don't be so silly—go back to bed,' my grandfather said after a moment or two, looking rather cross.

'No, it's true. He came and talked to me at the bottom of the bed. He told me he's not going to be sick any more.'

'Go back to bed,' my grandfather said, shooing me back up the stairs. 'Off you go!'

I slid back into bed and left my grandparents sitting up. As I lay there in the darkness, I knew exactly what I'd seen. I didn't need them to believe me.

As it turned out, they had sensed that I was telling the truth. I learned later that my mother and father had arrived home in the very early hours of the morning. Soon after I'd gone back to bed, they had telephoned to tell them that my grandad had passed over.

My mother had been devastated when my grandmother told her that I already knew. 'But we wanted to tell him,' she'd said, assuming my grandparents had woken me to tell me the news.

My grandmother had to tell her the truth. 'Oh no, we didn't tell him,' she said. 'He told us.'

My grandfather was as good as his word. During the mourning period and his funeral I had no sense of him being near me. I know now that this was because I was upset and grieving at the loss of someone who had played such a huge part in my young life. He was also going through the period of adjustment that all spirits go through when they

6

first cross over to the other side.

But as the pain faded and I began to remember him not with sadness but warmth he reappeared. Sometimes he would appear physically, at other times I would just be aware of his voice somewhere around me. Sometimes I would simply sense his kindly presence.

At first I didn't quite believe it. 'You can't be dead. You are here. I can see you, hear you, feel your presence,' I would say to him.

I didn't yet grasp that dead was the wrong word to use. I didn't yet understand that he was living another existence.

What was obvious to me, however, was that he was guiding me in some way.

*   *   *

I remember in the summer after he passed over I was walking home from school when I heard my grandfather's voice talking to me, somewhere behind me. There was an ambulance travelling at speed along the road, clearly on its way to or from some sort of emergency. 'Sonny Boy,' he said. 'See that ambulance—it's for your mum. You'd better run home.'

Sure enough when I got home the ambulance was outside the house. My mum had slipped and injured herself. The ambulance had been called and she was being taken to hospital for checks. It was quite serious but she made a full recovery.

I was still a young boy but it was at this point that I thought there had to be a reason for this. 'I am supposed to do something with this,' I thought to myself.

7

Over the course of that summer holiday my life began to change. First of all we moved home, to the three-bedroom, semi-detached house where my mum and dad still live today.

My grandad visited me again shortly before we moved. I had been a bit apprehensive about the move. Children like their routine and I didn't like the idea of having to change mine. Adding to my sense of foreboding, I was also about to start secondary school. My grandad told me that the house move and the change of school were going to be a big adventure for me. I was going to enjoy my new life. And so it proved.

I liked living at the new house and exploring the surrounding countryside. At my new school I quickly made new friends. It was a transforming moment in my life. I began to grow up.

As I did so, I felt more and more that there was a purpose to all this. I began to understand the reason why I could see and hear dead people. I was gifted with an ability to act as a medium, to translate and relay their thoughts and words, to help them communicate with people on this side of life.

So it was that in my teens I began to practise as a medium, communicating with other spirits at meetings and spiritualist church gatherings. When I was sixteen years old, I was taken to the Brighton Pavilion to see the late, great Doris Stokes, the woman who was the inspiration for me and every other modern psychic medium. I was fortunate enough to be invited backstage to meet her after the show. It was a big moment in my young life. From then on, the more I immersed myself in the mediumistic world, the more at home I felt there.

8

As I did so, my grandfather's presence slowly began to fade. He would visit me occasionally and I was aware of being in his company every now and again. But by the time I started working in earnest as a medium, in my late teens, he wasn't visiting any more. Our little chats had come to an end.

Once or twice I wondered whether this was because he didn't approve of what I was doing. Deep down I didn't believe that could be the case. After all, he was the one who had really opened the door to this new experience for me. I don't know if it happened by chance or whether my grandad 'organised' it, but before those doubts could grow, an encounter with a relative at a family funeral put my mind at rest.

'Hello, Colin,' the elderly man said, approaching me at the cemetery. He introduced himself as a cousin several times removed. 'You don't know me but I knew your grandad Lawrie very well.'

'Oh, yes,' I said, a bit uneasily.

'Yes. I know you're doing a lot of work as a medium now. Did you know that Lawrie used to be very interested in spiritualism?'

'No, I didn't,' I replied, slightly taken aback. It was the truth. We had talked a lot while he was alive, but Grandad had never mentioned anything about mediums, psychics, spiritualism or anything of that nature. I had no idea he had been actively interested.

'Oh yes. He kept it pretty quiet. You know what he was like. But he was very keen on it. Read a lot about it too. I think he'd have been very proud of what you're doing,' my cousin assured me.

Any doubts I'd had about why my grandad's presence had faded slipped away in an instant. I saw precisely what had happened. It wasn't that my grandad didn't approve of what I was doing. On the contrary. What I realised then was that, ever since that night when he'd passed over to the other side, my grandad had been trying to pass on a message to me. He had wanted to show me certain things, to explain certain truths to me. He had succeeded. Now, seeing that I was able to stand on my own two feet, he was going to leave me to act on that message. He had led me to the path my life was supposed to follow. It was now up to me to follow that path.

I still think of my grandfather regularly. Every now and again I will get the sense of his gentle presence somewhere around me. But I haven't seen or heard him since those distant, youthful days. What is so wonderful about what he taught me is that I don't miss him in the usual sense. I don't need to see or hear him any more. I don't need that sort of confirmation that he still exists. I simply know it.

*   *   *

The Message I received from my grandfather was the most significant and meaningful of my life. The truths it contained have guided me ever since.

He showed me that death is the greatest lie we are told. There is no such thing as death, only change. He showed me that the spirit world isn't like they taught us in Sunday school. He showed me that heaven is something that is not far, far away. It is near and close. It is what some people would call a parallel world. It's there and runs alongside us.

10

Most importantly of all, he showed me that while the end of his earthly life meant that he was separated from me, he was still around, still there for me to lean on when I needed him. And he showed me that if I carried on living my life with him in my mind and in my heart then he would always be there, ready to help and guide me.

Each of us faces the loss of a loved one at some time in our life. For most of us, it is the hardest thing we ever have to deal with emotionally. Whether it is the loss of a father or a friend, a mother or a brother, a son or a sister, it's sometimes an overwhelming experience, a time when it feels like our world is coming to an end.

And yet it isn't coming to an end. And nor is that of the one we have lost.

The loss of a loved one weakens us, but I believe it can make us stronger in the long term. I believe we can all give ourselves the hope and strength, not just to carry on with our earthly life, but to do so with a renewed sense of purpose and direction.

What is more, I believe that by continuing and growing within this earthly existence, we can all draw ourselves closer to the eternal life. We can all learn to keep those who have passed over to that parallel world near and close to ourselves. We can all understand the truth that my grandad passed on to me when I was a boy. We can all understand and receive the Message. This book will, I hope, show you how.

INTRODUCTION

Often, when I'm appearing at a live performance before large theatre audiences, locating the person with whom I am being asked to communicate by a spirit can be a slow process. It can take me a few minutes to make the connection, especially in larger venues, where there can be two thousand or more people gathered, some of them hidden high up in the balconies.

There were no such problems the night I felt the presence of a lady called Ruby during a performance in a theatre in the south of England. Almost immediately I mentioned the name, I saw an arm shooting up in the audience. I am always a little wary when I see someone react so quickly. Have they really heard enough information to be sure the connection is for them? Are they perhaps a little too eager to get a message from someone? But when I told the lady waving in the upper tier of the theatre that the woman communicating with me had beautiful, pale blue eyes she was even more convinced she knew who it was.

'Yes. That's my grandmother,' she said with complete certainty.

She proved to be absolutely right. As the connection solidified, I sensed a very strong character was channelling a message through me. Ruby was a fighter. She had been very ill in her late sixties, I sensed, but she had seen off her illness and lived on well into her eighties. Her granddaughter, Sarah, confirmed this.

Ruby had passed over a couple of years earlier.

13

During her earthly existence, she had been a woman who was fiercely independent, at least until the final few weeks of her life.

She also had a very modern sense of humour and was not easily shocked, as she proved as the reading progressed. Ruby was a very lively presence.

'I've got to tell you that she's very excited to be with you here tonight,' I told Sarah, who was sitting with other members of her family.

Ruby had a few messages she needed to get across to her daughter and her family in general. The first was a request that the family put three holly wreaths—two large ones and a smaller one—on a trio of graves that Christmas. She told me that it was a tradition that, through no fault of the family, had lapsed since she had passed over.

'She says it would be nice if you could start that again,' I told them. Sarah nodded in agreement.

The two most important communications came after this, however. Sitting next to Sarah was her daughter. Ruby asked to speak to her as well. As she did so her sense of humour shone through. Ruby told me that she had seen her great-granddaughter looking at saucy underwear in a shop. 'She is showing me something red and black,' I told her.

At this the young lady burst into fits of hysterical laughter. 'My boyfriend and I went to Ann Summers a few weeks ago,' she admitted, giggling away. 'We looked at this red and black basque.'

Unsurprisingly, this produced gales of laughter in the theatre. However, there was a serious point to this, I sensed.

'She says you shouldn't worry, our family has

14

childbearing hips,' I said. 'Do you understand that?'

This produced quiet nods from both Sarah and her daughter.

'Yes, we do,' they confirmed.

Then Ruby said she had a specific message for Sarah. 'To love once in your life is amazing, to love twice in your life means you are very blessed,' I said to Sarah.

'Yes,' she said. 'Thank you, Colin.'

Soon afterwards, a little reluctantly, Ruby faded away from me. The connection was over.

Afterwards, Sarah revealed that Ruby had died almost two years previously, during the Christmas holidays. She had Christmas dinner with the family but, being an independent spirit, had gone home. She had been found dead on Boxing Day, having suffered a massive heart attack. The thought that she had passed over on her own really devastated the family. Life had gone on for them. But they had never let their memories of their beloved nan fade. She remained in all their hearts.

It turned out that Sarah had come along for two very particular reasons. Her other daughter had been trying to conceive a child for a couple of years and was suffering from amongst other things a condition called endometriosis, which can stop the egg attaching itself to the side of the womb. The family was very worried that she might not be able to conceive. Sarah believed that Ruby's message about the 'childbearing hips' was a message of comfort for the family. She was telling them not to worry about it. Nature would find a way.

The second message related to Sarah's own life.

15

She had recently settled into a serious relationship with a new man in her life. She didn't spell out the details of what had happened in her previous relationship but it was clear that she had been badly burned and didn't want to be burned again.

'I wanted to know if I had made the right decision about my relationship,' she said afterwards. 'My nan answered both my questions.'

What was interesting about her was that she had visited another medium just days earlier. There too she'd been contacted by Ruby. On that occasion she'd been told that her nan had been standing next to her. She'd told her to fix her radiator, which had been leaking for two days. She also told her to check her boiler, which duly packed up shortly afterwards.

This lady clearly held her nan very close to her heart. She kept a photograph of her next to her bed. In the theatre tonight she was carrying a key ring with a photo of Ruby attached to it. The photograph was lovely and showed her at the centre of a family gathering, smiling radiantly.

*   *   *

I have chosen to begin this book with Ruby and Sarah not because the connection I made between them was particularly revealing. Compared to some of the many thousands of readings I have given during the thirty years I've been a medium, it was fairly undramatic. However, what was so wonderful about Sarah was the way that, in many ways, she summed up the Message I want to convey.

She and the rest of her family had clearly loved their grandmother very much. They had obviously been devastated by her loss and the manner in which she had passed over. I am sure there must have been some guilt over the way she had died on her own in the circumstances she did. But they had moved on with their lives. Sarah had found a new love in her life and her daughter was trying to have a baby.

And yet at the same time, Sarah and her family had always kept their nan in their minds and close to their hearts. They had acknowledged the sort of woman she was and how important she had been to her family. And as a result, Ruby had remained near, ready to guide them in times of need, as she had done that night.

Travelling around the world, I encounter many people who have this instinctive understanding of the Message. Without thinking about it or analysing it too much, they have lived their lives in a way that has kept them close to the spirit of the loved ones who have left this earthly existence. And they have been rewarded with a closeness and a connection that, at times, can seem almost as natural as those they have with relatives they ring on the telephone, or contact by text or email.

In many ways, connecting with the other side is a communication skill to be learned. In the same way that we can feel the presence of those close to us on this earthly plane by picking up the phone or sitting at the computer and sending them an email, it is possible to receive—and send—messages to the other side. The key to it lies in how we live our lives after those loved ones leave this earthly existence. This is the Message I want to convey in this book.

This book is divided into seven parts, beginning

with the acknowledgement of our grief when a loved one passes over, and moving on to a place where we can experience the continuing connection with our loved ones ourselves. Each part is designed as an important step along the way on the journey from pain and loss to hope and healing. Dealing with and moving on from the death of a loved one can be a difficult and, at times, an overwhelming process. But we can all heal ourselves and forge ahead in life with a renewed sense of direction and purpose. And by doing so we can make those who have passed over feel closer to us rather than farther away.

PART ONE

Acknowledgement

Only by acknowledging them, can you move on. And only by moving on can you discover them again.

A New Existence

When someone passes over they begin a new existence. They leave behind the earthly life and enter the spirit world.

Yet they are not the only ones for whom a new existence is beginning.

The first thing we need to understand is that when we lose someone important in our lives, we are turning the pages of a new chapter in the story of our own existence as well.

Passing through this phase of our life isn't going to be easy. It is going to be a very intense time. We are going to experience very powerful feelings, emotions and thoughts. It is, at times, going to feel overwhelming. But we must understand this: it is only one part of our existence, one stage of our life experience. It is only a part of the big picture.

It is vital that, at this early stage, we understand that there is great purpose in why we feel things emotionally and intellectually during this stage of our existence. It is a crucial and natural part of our development as human beings. We must also understand that we are going to view the world very differently from now on.

Again, our earthly experience is going to mirror the one our loved one is going through in the spirit dimension. When we pass over into the spirit dimension, our personality doesn't change and our character doesn't change. What does change is the way we sense and experience the emotions and thought processes. We are existing on a higher, faster, lighter plane. We evolve.

In many senses, the same applies here in our earthly existence. When we go through a major bereavement, when someone very important to us passes over, our way of interpreting and feeling the earthly world around us changes fundamentally. People who are dealing with someone's passing often say the world feels like a different place now that they aren't here. Well, that's true. It is a different world because we are seeing and experiencing it differently.

One of the best ways of understanding how we experience this different form of existence is to think back to our childhoods. Try to imagine how you thought about things when you were a child. Picture, if you can, how you felt about your mother or your siblings. Try to see in your mind's eye how you viewed the world around you. It was a very different perspective, wasn't it? It seemed a very different place. You didn't see anything in the same context as you do today, did you?

It is the same now. You are still the same person, of course. But your emotions, feelings and thoughts bear no comparison to those you felt when you were as a child. You've evolved, you've grown, you've become something more. But fundamentally you're still the same person.

This is how I try to encourage people to think. Life has moved on for us as it has for those who have passed over. They too are experiencing their new existence in a way that is different from the one they knew here on the earthly plane. We must all move on in this new existence.

*   *   *

When I begin to feel the presence of someone on the spirit side trying to make a connection, my head can initially be filled with a bewildering jumble of sights, sounds and thoughts—even smells. It invariably takes a while for me to form a clear picture of who and what I am being shown. So it proved with this lady as she came through to me one evening. At first I had the impression that she had taken her own life. But as the barrage of information she was showing me began to become clearer, I understood that she had in fact chosen to slip away from life, as a great many elderly and very sick people so often do.

It was clear that she had been very ill throughout her final days. My mind was filled with images of bottles of drugs, kaolin and morphine, in particular. I could sense her almost secretly drinking the kaolin and morphine, against all her doctor's and family's wishes. I got the sense that she had been a rather sad and depressed lady towards the end. I began to form an image of someone who had been restless to leave this earthly life, someone who wanted to get over to the other side.

I managed to connect her to a lady in the audience who turned out to be one of her daughters. She confirmed the details I'd relayed so far. She explained that she and her mum had been due to fly off on holiday together. However, the lady had died quite suddenly and unexpectedly the day before they were due to travel.

Her mother was anxious to apologise for this. 'She says she gave up and she's sorry about that,' I said. Her daughter accepted the apology, quietly nodding.

As the connection continued, the lady showed

me why it was that she had been so keen to pass over. She had never recovered from the loss of her husband. 'The day they took my fella away in a box my life over there ended,' she said.

'That's very true,' her daughter said, holding back tears now.

Her mother's main message, however, was that her daughter shouldn't be worrying about her. She wanted her to know that her existence was continuing on the spirit side. Not just that, it was a happier existence than she'd had on this side during her final months.

She did not mention her husband. I sensed that her passing was still quite recent and it may well have been that they hadn't been reunited as yet. She was still passing through the period of adjustment our loved ones seem to go through when they pass over.

But it was clear that she was relishing her existence on the other side, not least because she had completely recovered her personality. As her daughter listened to her talking through me, I could see the smile spreading across her face as she too recognised this. This was the mother she remembered from earlier in her earthly life, not the rather sombre person she had known at the end of her days here. Her mother had got her sense of humour back. She was her old self again.

She was even able to get an answer to a question that had been worrying her. Her family had been squabbling over the wedding ring her mother had left behind. The lady told her daughter to go to a favourite bridge of theirs and toss it into the water below. This made her laugh out loud. She promised to do it, however.

By the time the connection came to an end her mother had brought a huge smile to the lady's face. It was as if a great weight had been lifted off her shoulders. It was a simple message, typical of the many I have relayed over the years. It put the lady's mind at rest that her mother had indeed passed over to another existence, one where she was at peace with herself once more. It rid her of the guilt she had felt about the circumstances of her mother's passing. And it freed her to concentrate on the most important thing on this earthly side, re-adjusting to life without her mother.

In that sense, it contained a lesson we can all draw upon. There is nothing we can do about the experience our loved ones go through as they set off on the new journey that begins when they pass over. We must, for a while, leave them to it. What we can do in the meantime, however, is concentrate on the beginning of our own journey. And that means coming to terms with their passing by first grieving properly and then acknowledging the person whose earthly presence we miss so much.

Grieving for Ourselves

As we learn to live in this very different and new emotional environment, it is important that we understand and examine grief itself.

What is grief? What is its purpose? Why are we grieving? Who are we grieving for?

Let me answer that last question first. The answers to the other questions lie within it. When you sit down and think about it, we are actually grieving for ourselves. We are feeling a sense of loss that the physical side of our loved one is gone. We are missing the touch of them, the feel of them, the conversations we used to share with them. Those things have all gone.

And it has left us floundering, asking ourselves, 'How will I cope now that I can no longer sense those things? How will I carry on now that I can't hear their words of comfort when I need to be comforted?' This is what grief is and why we grieve. We are re-adjusting to the circumstances of our physical life. We are mourning the physical change that has occurred in our earthly lives. When you boil it down, that is what we are grieving for. Our belief that a physical presence has gone. But has it?

The world is telling you that your beloved husband, wife, son, daughter, mother, father, friend, is dead. They are telling you that is the absolute truth. And it is, to an extent. The fact that the physical presence is not there is undeniable.

But is there not something of them left in this physical world? Look around you and you will find the answer is obvious. Yes, there is.

The most obvious way of doing this is by turning to your family. If your husband, wife or partner has passed on and you have children, you can look at them and immediately see something of them there. It is there in their physical appearance, in their mannerisms, their smile.

Or let's say your parent passes over. Take a look at yourself. How many of us have found ourselves coming out with that expression, 'Oh, I'm beginning to sound like my father or my mother?' Quite a few of us.

We do so because it's true. We do reach a point in our lives when we realise that everything that was in our dad or our mum is now in us. And when they pass over it doesn't die with them. It lives on in us. If you look inside yourself you can find everything that you feel you are going to miss in them. Everything of them is in you.

The same principle applies regardless of your connection with the person who has passed over, whether it is a blood relationship or not. Your friends and partners have left something of themselves within you. There are things that you shared together that live on inside your memory, your heart. They are present there still.

So this is the first truth you need to decide on. Is their presence really no longer around? If you decide that in fact something of that person has carried on, you can move on with that thought safely placed in your mind. And as you do so you can, in time, evolve your new life so that you are able to embrace something more than just a physical presence. You can keep another more spiritual connection alive.

Never Say Never: Setting the Right Pattern

It is, of course, human to feel pain, particularly the pain of the loss of a loved one. Pain is healthy, and we should experience it. It is important that we do so.

We do, however, have to be careful about something. It is vitally important at this point that we do not set a pattern that stops us from ever moving on.

Let me give you an example of what I mean

here. People can say very dramatic things at this painful stage in the process. But they can also say things that are going to tie them down, constrain them. I have heard many recently bereaved people, for instance, say things like:

'I am never going to get over this.'
'I cannot live without this person.'
'As far as I'm concerned my life has ended now.'

They are very common statements, but they are also dangerous because if we allow these thoughts to set the pattern or template for what lies ahead then we won't ever get over our grief. And if we don't do that we won't be able to re-establish our connection with our loved ones in the spirit world.

So what do you say? How do you express that mixture of anger, regret and sadness that goes to make up your grief? You do need to express it. So how do you do it?

The key is to set a pattern in your mind. You must tell yourself: 'This is my time to grieve, this is my time to feel sorrow for the lack of touch and comfort and company and physical presence. I am allowed to have this moment of pain. It is my pain and I'm entitled to it. And I'm entitled to experience it.'

But at the same time as you are experiencing that pain it is important you set up other patterns in your mind. You must also say to yourself: 'I know this period is going to be hard. But I also know that life will go on. Both for me and the person, or persons, for whom I am grieving. And I know that I am going to come to terms with this.'

If you do that, you will have set a pattern that

will allow you to move on when the time comes.

What you are doing here is giving yourself the time to grieve over the circumstances of their passing. As I said earlier, that's what grieving is all about, missing what we feel we have lost by the termination of a physical life.

Once you have dealt with that you can begin to consider what steps you need to take to continue your relationship with them, to keep them alive within you.

Living Your Experience

We experience a huge variety of emotions when we lose someone we love. For many of us, the pain is immense. It seems unbearable.

But some of us feel the exact opposite of pain. We feel relief, joy, sometimes even elation. I have encountered people whose reaction to loss has been closer to ecstasy than agony. In some cases, this was because they understood the Message, the fact that existence continues after this physical life.

I remember one lady I encountered at a charity event I was attending. She started talking to me about an aunt she had just lost. She was very close to this lady who had clearly been a big influence in her life.

Over a glass of wine, the lady told me in no uncertain terms that she was incredibly pleased that her aunt had passed over.

'I'm actually really glad for her,' she told me. 'Best thing that could have happened to her actually. She was a very active, intelligent woman and had a led a very long, very full life. But she had come to the point where her body wasn't doing what she wanted it to do. Her mind was going too. She was getting forgetful and a little bit clumsy around the house. This was making her cross with herself. I wasn't sure of it, but I wouldn't have been surprised if it was the start of dementia.'

She continued, 'So I'm delighted for her because this part of her life has come to an end and she can get on with the next part of it now.'

I've also come across people who were happy because they were relieved that their loved one's suffering had come to an end.

Another lady I met once, this time at a party organised by some friends, described to me how she'd felt this immense wave of happiness wash over her when her husband had passed.

He had suffered a long-drawn-out illness and had spent an inordinate amount of time being shuttled in and out of hospitals. He had had numerous operations and treatments, none of which, ultimately, had changed things. He had borne it stoically, but it had been an awful time for him—and his wife and their family.

'He experienced so much pain towards the end of his life that I cried tears of joy when he finally passed over,' the lady told me. 'I was so ecstatic because at last he was free of it. He was free of the pain and the indignity and the suffering of it all. No one should have to go through that.'

Of course, having such strong views can cause friction, particularly in families, and so it had proved in this lady's case. The rest of her family didn't understand her at all. They thought her behaviour after her husband's death was somehow wrong, almost disrespectful of him. It was as if they expected her to play the archetypal grieving widow, draped in black with a veil over her head. They completely failed to see why she could be so overjoyed at the loss. But I didn't. I understood her completely.

In my experience, far too many people are weighed down with guilt for harbouring such feelings. Unlike the two ladies I've mentioned here, they walk around castigating themselves, feeling awful because they aren't more upset than they are at someone's passing.

'I should be feeling pain not happiness. What's wrong with me?' they say to themselves. Well, the answer is nothing is wrong with you.

Whenever I meet someone who feels this way I always say the same thing: you don't *have* to feel pain at the loss of someone. You don't have to feel anything just because somebody else says you should.

Nobody has the right to tell you what you should feel.

Compassion Not Sympathy

As we move through this process of grief it is important we surround ourselves with the right messages. We have told ourselves that we will allow ourselves a time for grieving but that life *will* go on afterwards. We need to be surrounded by people who are echoing this.

People are going to react to you in several different ways when you experience a major bereavement.

Some people simply aren't comfortable around death. They may not have faced it before or they may have struggled to deal with it themselves in

30

the past. Some of these will give you a wide berth altogether. It doesn't reflect greatly on them as friends, but we shouldn't think too badly of them for doing this.

Others will be impatient and intolerant of your feelings. Others will say things that they believe are helping but are only intensifying your pain. Some will say things like: 'Get over it.' 'Get a grip of yourself.' Others will turn up immediately and start delivering platitudes like: 'Don't worry—you've still got your looks, you'll find someone else,' Or: 'You're young enough, you can still have another child.' Those are the last things you need to hear at the moment, even if they are said with the best of intentions.

More often than not, however, people will offer you one of two things: sympathy and compassion. It might seem that these are both welcome. They are not, however.

There is a huge difference between sympathy and compassion. The best way I can think of to describe it is this. If you were up to your neck in quicksand and a kind-looking man came along, saw you and simply said, 'I feel really sorry for the predicament you are in,' before walking on, that would be sympathy. If, on the other hand, someone came along, saw the trouble you were in and then tried to pull you out, that would be compassion. There is a great difference between the two. We must all seek out compassion and not sympathy during this time.

The last thing anybody needs when they lose someone is sympathy. When we are at our lowest, the worst thing we can get is those silly cards people send marked 'in loving sympathy'. It reminds me of that old phrase 'tea and sympathy' which, to me, is another way of saying tea and misery. It conjures up memories of people sitting around, ashen faced, muttering away about how hard it must be for you, how much you are going to miss your loved one, how empty the house feels without their presence. That is the last thing you need to hear.

What we really need is compassion. What we need is someone to come along and say: 'OK, this has happened and it's terrible. Now let's see how we can help each other along.'

We want someone who will come along and ask us: 'What do you need in the next hour to take you forward from what you are feeling now?'

We want someone who will then say: 'If we can work out what you need in the next hour we can move on to work out what you need in the next week. And from that into the next year.'

That's what we all need. And we should embrace everyone who provides it.

Bereavement Burnout

A great many people fill their lives with things so that they don't have to dwell on their bereavement or remember the person who has passed over. 'As long as I keep myself busy I don't have to think about them,' they tell themselves. 'If I fill my life full of events, work, my children, my grandchildren, whatever, my grief will go away.'

This is misguided. We shouldn't fill our lives with things simply so that we can forget.

Why not? Well, you may find you can achieve this for a period of time. You may find that you can

32

fill your life with the meaningless repetition of working twenty-four hours a day or partying like there is no tomorrow. But it will catch up with you. You will eventually reach a point of bereavement burnout. And when that day comes you will realise that all this stuff you've been doing hasn't actually helped you come to terms with the fact this person has passed over at all. Nor has it made you feel any closer to them. In fact, in your private moments you are still grieving as much as ever. So you have in effect got nowhere.

You must spend time going through the grieving process. If you don't do it now, you are only postponing it for another day.

Consoling and Counselling

Trying to come to terms with the passing of someone who has been close to us is a very personal and individual experience. Intense grief can last for months or even years.

It is probable that you are going to experience one, some or all of five distinct emotions. Again, everyone's experience is going to be different; you cannot put a time scale on when, how or even in what order you are going to feel these things. The emotions can come in short succession or be spread over a long period. Usually they consist of:

Shock
The feeling of being disconnected from anything and everything and being totally unable to comprehend what has happened.

Distress and despair
The heartbreaking feeling of loss.

Guilt
The feeling that you should have done more for the loved one that has passed over.

Anger
This can be expressed in a multitude of directions. You may feel angry with the loved one who has passed over for having left you. You might be angry at those who have survived. You might be angry with yourself.

Bitterness
This is often directed at other people who seem to be able to cope better or are happier than yourself. The first thing to say is that it is so important to acknowledge that these are normal human emotions at this time of grief. Nonetheless they are damaging and dark feelings. For your own sake, the sake of your earthly friends and family as well as those who have moved on to the higher life, you need to find a way to move on from them in time.

Everyone—from our nearest and dearest to the lady at the corner shop—will have a view about how we should be going about our grieving. Initially of course everyone will be very kind and caring. But after a while we will start to hear the inevitable suggestion: 'You should be over this by now.' This is hardly helpful, especially when we are still in a position where we aren't able to see the wood for the trees emotionally.

Accepting the consolation of friends and family is, of course, extremely comforting. Often it is all that is required to enable us to move on and start to live again without the physical presence of a loved one or friend. But there will always be those who find the consoling words and deeds of family and friends only seem to underline their sense of loss. What should these people do? Where should they turn for help, guidance and the compassion they need?

You may be surprised when I say that, initially, rushing to see a medium is not always the answer in some cases.

In the days when I undertook far more one-to-one private sittings than I am able to do now, I usually had one sitting a week with a person who was still in the throes of deep grief. My advice was for them to go away and rethink if this was the course of action they wanted to undertake. Often it wasn't.

In these cases my instinct is that the preferable option at this stage is a period of professional counselling. This is not to say, I hasten to add, that seeing a medium may not be possible later on. Of course, that may well be an option you will want to follow. But I think it is often right to begin with a counsellor.

Although there are many bereavement counsellors who wouldn't approve of people seeking the services of mediums, that doesn't detract from the fact that mediums often do good work. As a medium I believe that bereavement counselling and the services of a good medium can work hand in hand in supporting a person through their time of grief. Although friends and family can be kind and supporting, their love and compassion can sometimes become a grief trap. It doesn't help you move away from this feeling of despair that lives deep within you.

However, by rushing to see a medium too soon you can run the risk of becoming message obsessed. I have seen this happen too. People start seeking more and more messages to eliminate their sense of loss. They aren't dealing with that sense of loss or moving on with their lives at all. This is not the reason you should be seeking to see a medium and quite frankly any medium worth their salt should explain this to you. Our function is not just to give you evidence of your loved one's continuing existence beyond physical death. It is also to play our part in enabling you to continue your life in a positive way.

Good professional counselling will give you an opportunity to talk about your grief with a neutral third party who can guide you towards a path of renewed life.

The good thing about this is that if you then also see a medium, should you get a connection with your loved one, you are going to be armed with many of the tools you are going to need to get on with your life. You will also receive any messages that come through in the right way, treating them not as a means to heal your broken heart but as a way of receiving further evidence of your friend's or loved one's continuing love.

You might be asking yourself, 'When should I go for counselling?' The answer is that there is no time scale with regards to counselling, no set time when it should begin or when it should end. Obviously, many will seek this as an option quite soon after a bereavement. But it is also possible that you may feel the need to resolve these issues many years after the passing of a loved one. Whenever you go for counselling, it's vital that you don't feel guilty about needing help. Most bereavement counselling services are well experienced with all the different circumstances and situations of grief. They are not there to judge you—nor will they.

It's worth pointing out that organisations such as Cruse and Compassionate Friends, two of the major bereavement counselling services, are voluntarily run and therefore have waiting lists. So you will need to be patient. You can find your local branch of these organisations in the telephone directory or on the internet.

Seeking Your Truth: the Act of Acknowledgement

Dealing with the passing of a loved one is ultimately a personal experience. No matter how much help, support, compassion and care we get from others, it is, in the end, a journey we must complete on our own. We have to manage the experience personally. We have to reach an accommodation with what has happened on our own terms.

This is something we must accept. So at this point we have to understand that it's no good screaming at the world. There is no value in lashing out and shouting: 'You don't understand, you don't know what I'm going through.'

What we are saying is absolutely right, of course. It's a matter of fact. The rest of the world doesn't understand what we are going through. How could they? This is our personal experience. Well, almost.

The one other person who really can be involved

in the process in a meaningful and active way is the person who has caused this pain, the loved one who has left this earthly existence for the spirit world. They are at the heart of the first part of our journey.

We must begin by acknowledging them and what they mean to us.

* * *

How do we begin the process of coming to terms with someone's passing? How do we take the first step towards living the new existence that awaits us? How do we do this in a way that ensures that we can feel their presence again further down the road?

Well, the first thing we need to face up to is the truth about the person we are grieving. And by that I mean our own, personal truth—what that person meant to us as individuals. I call this the act of acknowledgement. To achieve this we each need to ask ourselves some key questions.

- What was the true nature of my relationship with that person?
- What were they really like?
- How did I really feel about them?
- How did they inspire me or how did they fail to inspire me?
- How do I carry on with that inspiration?
- How do I overcome any negative aspects that my relationship with them may have contained?

This part of the process requires us to be painfully honest with ourselves. We must look deep inside.

It is not enough just to say that 'they meant so much to me because they were my husband, my daughter, my best friend,' or whatever. You have to make an honest appraisal of why that relationship was so important.

So the act of acknowledgement is about looking for the deeper things that a person brought into our lives. It is about analysing why we loved them, what it was about their personality and character that made them special to us. Was it their sense of fun, of fairness or adventure perhaps? Their willingness to laugh at themselves or to see good in others maybe?

It is also about examining their influence on us. How did their presence inspire us or how did their presence fail to inspire us?

It is about then asking how do we carry on with that inspiration? Or if they weren't that kind of influence and held us back in life how do we move on from that?

This might require some awkward questions. It's about being really honest with yourself about the true nature of your relationship with the person who has passed over.

If, for instance, you had a daughter who passed over with whom you had an intense relationship, you must explore why it was intense. It wasn't just because she was your daughter—because many mothers and daughters don't get on, many fathers and sons don't get on. It's making an honest appraisal of the particular, unique circumstances that explain why that relationship meant so much to you.

Was the person who has passed over controlling, perhaps? Did they make all the decisions? If so, how are you going to now take up the reins?

It may be something as simple as your wife having done all the cooking, or paying all the bills. You may never have had to do those things so you may have to take inspiration from who your wife was and what she did in this respect.

In that case you can be inspired by the fact that you must learn to do all the things she used to do. And by learning to do those things you learn to become closer to her.

Whatever it was that defined that person and their role in our lives, we all have to discover the pure truth. Only then will we be able to look at that truth, draw something from it and learn how it can help us move on.

Looking to Yourself for Answers

I knew this lady was going to be hard work the moment she stepped into my office. It was as if she'd come for a business meeting.

She was about thirty-five years old and was dressed in a blue, pinstripe skirt and jacket. When I invited her to sit down she sat there cross-legged with a notebook in her hand. To be honest she was one of those people who make me wonder why on earth they have come to see me.

For a moment or two, as I weighed her up, I wondered whether she might even be a newspaper reporter that was trying to catch me out. For this reason, I was on my guard at first.

As the reading got under way, however, I began to relax. I made a strong connection with a lady. 'I know this lady is your mother,' I said.

'Yes,' the woman said, coolly making a note, as if

taking dictation from her boss.

'I know she has passed in the last eighteen months.'

'Yes, that's right.'

'She is showing me the importance of the name Maureen, so I believe her name is Maureen.'

She just kept nodding and making notes and saying: 'Yes, that's right.'

After a while, however, the picture started to get a bit more complicated. 'I'm really confused by something she's showing me,' I said. 'You live in a house that is overlooking a duck pond.'

'Yes, that's right.'

'This is peculiar. Your mother is showing me that you are trying to get a mortgage but you are not moving,' I said.

She sat there quietly.

'Ah, you are renting at the moment but want to buy.'

'Yes, that's right.'

'And yet I know from what your mother is showing me that you are not happy about this. You really don't want to buy this house.'

Again this produced nothing but a rather heavy silence.

'Your mother is saying there are other options.'

I've seen a lot in my years as a medium, but I don't think I've ever quite seen a reaction like the one I saw when I told her this. All of a sudden her impassive, business-like exterior disappeared. She slammed down the notepad and looked almost ready to explode with rage.

'Hah, that is absolutely typical of my mother!' she said. 'Full of bright ideas, but no bloody answers.'

41

I was taken aback a little by this. There were clearly some very serious issues between this lady and her mother. But I was also a little annoyed with her behaviour. It showed very little appreciation of the effort I—and more importantly—her mother were putting into this reading.

'Hang on a minute, love,' I said, trying to calm her. 'Your mother has made a huge effort to get through to you today. Don't you think you should be a bit more appreciative of the effort she has made to get through?'

'Well,' she said, slightly apologetically. 'My mother and I weren't very close.'

I suspended the reading for a moment so we could talk. She started telling me what had happened.

When she had died, the mother had left her house to her sister, leaving this lady with her life savings instead. She had clearly been a well organised woman and had also understood money. Both had been left very well cared for by her will. It seemed like even this was not enough, however.

As we talked the lady remained bitter and angry. 'Why can't she tell me what the other options are?' she asked me.

'Because you have free will and you have to make choices in your life,' I explained.

She simply grunted and shrugged her shoulders as if this was a concept she didn't want to face.

'Your mother left you her life savings, for goodness' sake. Isn't that enough?' I continued.

'No,' she said bluntly.

At that point I terminated the sitting.

I was not surprised that the woman seemed so

tense and uptight. She was still in the throes of grieving her mother. She hadn't even begun to acknowledge her importance to her. If she had, she would have been seeing things completely differently.

She didn't seem to understand how good her mother had been to her. Clearly she had organised and looked after her daughters financially. The way she had divided up her will was an indicator of that.

But it was obvious she had also been an emotional crutch for her daughter as well. With that crutch now kicked away from under her, her daughter was clearly unable to stand on her own two feet. She had turned her anger against her mother. Completely inappropriately in my view.

She still expected her to provide all the answers in life.

The irony, of course, was that if the daughter had acknowledged her mother she would have provided her with answers. She had proven that by coming through for her daughter in the reading.

'It was you she came through to, not your sister,' I told the lady. 'Can't you see any significance in that?'

'No,' she said again.

As she left I felt genuinely sorry for the lady. She wasn't prepared to move forward and make some decisions to advance her own life. The biggest decision she had to make was to acknowledge her mother. She needed to sit down and think deeply about what her mother had done for her and what she had meant to her.

She needed to acknowledge the person who had left such a large gap in her life. The irony was that, if she had done it sooner, she may well have been given the answers she was looking for.

Sidestep the Circumstances

For many of us, acknowledging the true nature of our relationship with the person who has passed over is difficult because of the circumstances of their departure.

If their passing was the result of a terrible, debilitating illness, an accident, the result of misadventure, a suicide, or—perhaps worst of all— as the consequence of a violent act, those circumstances can be hard to put to one side. But they have to be put to one side. They have to be sidestepped.

Hard as it might be, we have to try to separate ourselves from the circumstances because that's what often causes the most intense aspect of our grief.

If we want to acknowledge the person who has passed over, if we want to be able to answer the series of all-important questions I outlined above, we have to do this. We have to remember the real person that we knew for many years, not dwell on the person they became at the end of this earthly existence.

Often this part of the process is dealt with best when we sit down and really think about the inspiration the person who has passed over provided in our lives. As I have seen many times, the impact this has can be hugely cathartic.

Let me give you a couple of examples that, hopefully, illustrate what I mean here.

The experience of two ladies who had to deal

with extremely difficult circumstances illustrates the point in very different ways.

*   *   *

A few years ago I did a private reading for a lady who lived near Liverpool. Her name was Anne. Arriving for the session, Anne seemed very calm, serene and generally very pleasant. I sensed she was quite a happy woman at heart. But I could also feel that there had been some great sadness in her life.

When the reading began, I quite quickly made a connection with a man who seemed to be trying to get in contact with Anne. I sensed he had passed over in very sudden, violent circumstances.

It turned out to be her husband, Ronnie.

The reading was quite short but extremely powerful. He wanted to let her know that he was all right and that he loved her. But there was one message that he was really pushing me to get across to Anne.

'I don't know if you will understand this, but your husband is telling me that he thinks the greatest thing you did was to forgive that man,' I told her. 'Does that mean anything?'

'Yes, it does,' she said, her composure suddenly gone as she began dabbing away at her eyes.

'And he is telling me that the fact you did it to his face made it an even greater thing,' I went on.

'Yes,' Anne said quietly.

He ended his message by telling her that he was very, very proud of what she had done.

'Thank you,' she said at the end of the reading. 'That's what I travelled all this way hoping to hear.'

As we chatted afterwards, she told me the

terrible story that lay behind this.

A year or so earlier Ronnie had been walking home from work, just as he did every night of the week. On this particular night, however, he had been jumped on by a man with a knife. The attacker had stabbed him, snatched his briefcase and then run off leaving Ronnie lying bleeding in the street. By the time the emergency services had come to his aid, he had bled to death.

It was a hideous crime, made even more awful by the fact that the thief had escaped with a briefcase which contained nothing more than £20 and a pocket calculator.

Ronnie's death had devastated Anne, naturally. She had, like so many people who suffer a loss like this, felt a mixture of shock, anger and hatred towards the perpetrator. He had destroyed not only the life of a loving husband, but hers and that of Ronnie's family too. Ronnie's killer was beyond contempt, as far as she was concerned.

The crime shocked the local community and the police were quickly able to arrest the man responsible. He was brought to trial and found guilty. He was sentenced to life in prison.

Anne attended the trial, even though it brought back such harrowing memories. It took a lot of courage to do so, she admitted to me.

She was there at the end when the judge sentenced her husband's killer to life in jail. But it was at the climax of the legal process, when others would have been rejoicing in the fact that justice had been done, that she did something that acknowledged Ronnie and the kind of man he was.

'As he was being taken out of the court he turned and looked at me,' she said. 'He had this

46

real pleading look on his face. I knew what it meant. He wanted me to forgive him.'

Anne was honest enough to admit that it was not in her make-up to do that. Ronnie, however, had been different. Anne had spent enough time thinking about Ronnie and the kind of man he was to know that he would have been able to forgive.

So as the killer was led down into the cells beneath the courtroom, Anne looked at him and mouthed the three words he was begging her to say: 'I forgive you.'

'I believe that was what Ronnie would have wanted me to do,' she told me. 'That was his attitude, not mine. But I have almost had to take on his attitude to life and think that even the unforgivable should be forgiven.

'I said those words because I knew that unless I did I would never have moved on with my life,' she told me. 'I am trying to be more like him. I am trying to keep his spirit alive.'

She left happy, knowing that she had done the right thing. Ronnie had approved of her actions. And she had kept his spirit alive.

Anne's story illustrates how the act of acknowledgement can help even the most painful losses to become more bearable. And it illustrates too how we can keep the spirit of the person we have lost alive in ourselves.

But it is also a great illustration of how before we can do either of those things, we must sidestep the circumstances of our loss.

It is, I think, an inspiring story, and one we should all keep in mind.

*　　*　　*

The moment I began to sense the man connecting with me I immediately sensed some sort of violent death. There was something unusual about it, however. I could see the figure of someone who had passed over while in an awkward, unnatural position, neither standing nor sitting.

When a young lady sitting in the audience identified herself she confirmed it was her father.

'Would you understand that he was neither standing nor sitting?'

'Yes, I would. He died on his knees,' she said. She was relatively young, in her late twenties to thirties, I'd guess. She was very composed and calm, despite the sense of tragedy that I could feel around her father's passing.

I also sensed a great air of mystery about the circumstances. I got the impression of an air of confusion, of questions swirling around him.

'Nobody has been able to account for the mark or bruise on the side of his head,' I said.

'No, no one has been able to explain it,' the young lady said.

'And there were several investigations. The coroner had to look at this case three times and the police investigated it twice,' I said.

'Yes, that's right,' she confirmed.

'There was also something strange about £2,200 that had either been put in or taken out of a bank account.'

'Yes,' she said.

It was the next piece of information that clarified what had happened a little more.

'I am sensing that there was a length of cord or rope or that someone tried to strangle him,' I said.

'Yes, he hung himself,' she said, again quite calmly.

The gravity of the story was, by now, becoming clear. So too was the fact that this man was trying to get some important messages through.

I found it quite difficult to translate the next sentence. When I eventually got it out, I felt myself almost stuttering. 'F-f-frightened for my own safety. What I did was the easiest option,' I said.

'Do you understand that?' I said.

'Yes. I do,' the girl said.

This was clearly a soul who was desperate to communicate with those he'd left behind on this earthly plane. It had already been a powerful message, but there was still more to come.

'Please tell Mum I can now stand proud because I know I did no wrong.'

'Yes,' the lady nodded.

'I am also being shown an engagement ring,' I said. It looked rather like a ring that I had myself, in white gold with stones of some kind, possibly diamonds, encrusted in the side. 'You're getting engaged,' I said to the young lady.

'No. Not me. It's my mum. My mum just got engaged,' she replied.

This produced a real wave of emotion in the man coming through to me. There was almost a sense of elation in his thoughts. 'He is saying to me: "to see her get married would be the greatest thing I could ever wish for."'

'Yes,' the lady smiled.

As his connection faded, I told her what he was placing in my mind. 'He is thanking you for all the kindness after he was found dead in such peculiar circumstances.'

49

I realised that this had been a very powerful and significant message and so it proved when she spoke after the reading. The lady explained that her dad had been found dead in his garden shed. He was kneeling with a rope around his neck.

'My dad passed away on New Year's morning,' she said.

She had called him and spoken to him briefly just after midnight. 'I had a feeling that something was not quite right,' she explained. She phoned the police and found them at his house when she arrived there. 'We had to break into the house,' she said.

The £2,200 referred to some money that was put into her account and then mysteriously was bounced. It was clearly a very significant moment for the young lady. But what impressed me about her was the fact that she had been so composed throughout.

It was clear to me that this must have been the most horrendous experience for her. The impact on her must have been immense. Not only had her father taken his own life, something that can often produce feelings of guilt in those who remain. But she had been the last person to speak to him.

In the wake of his death, her mind must have been a maelstrom of conflicting emotions. She must have been bedevilled with questions: *Why didn't I talk to him for longer, try to find out what he was thinking? Why didn't I get round there quicker? Why didn't I tell the police to hurry?*

She must have been through a terrible ordeal. Many other people would still have been eaten up by that mix of anger, regret, guilt and confusion that comes when someone takes their own life.

Yet, as she had proven, she had come through it all. She had acknowledged, in a very straightforward way, that her father had taken his own life. He had been involved in something that required a police investigation. But she had not dwelt on it. She had sidestepped the circumstances and embraced the truth of who her real father was. He was a caring, warm-hearted man who, for tragic reasons, had been driven to take his own life.

'I feel him with me quite often but this is the first time he has come through. Now I know he is there I am really happy,' she said.

Her connection underlined to me something fundamental to the Message I believe we should all understand.

If we put aside the circumstances, no matter how painful and complex and riddled with guilt and mystery they may be, if we acknowledge the person for who they are and move on with our lives, then, some day, somehow, they will find a way to get through to us. Just as this lady's father had.

Remember Them as They Were—and Are

Illness can take a terrible toll, not just on the person who is suffering but on their loved ones too. Watching someone we love go through a long and painful decline can have a profound effect on us, the ones who are left behind in this life. When that person has passed it can be hard to replace the memory of the final, difficult days with a happier, more positive memory.

One way of thinking about it is by imagining the journey that our loved ones are continuing on in the afterlife. Remember, those who have passed over are getting on with a new existence. They are moving on. If we keep moving in our existence then we will stay in closer contact. Stay still and we will lose touch, move on with our lives and they will remain near. By thinking this way we can begin not just to erase the most painful images but also free up those happy memories of the earthly life we shared with them before their passing.

A communication intended for a lady in Kent, while I was giving a show in a coastal town there, illustrates this point.

There were several hundred people in the auditorium at the time, but the lady, named Amanda, quickly recognised this person was trying to make contact with her. I was glad she did. I hadn't had a clue why I'd been shown Jimmy Savile and his show *Jim'll Fix It*.

Amanda did immediately. She had always wanted to be famous and had watched that show and *Opportunity Knocks*, dreaming of appearing on one of them. She had gone so far as auditioning for *Opportunity Knocks*. She guessed it might be her father trying to make contact and was even more sure of it when I said I sensed his passing had been within the past year or so. As it turned out, that night was the first anniversary of his passing.

Ralph's humour came through in the connection. At one point, for instance, he apologised that his funeral cost £270 more than it should have!

But he had a very specific message for his daughter.

Ralph showed me that he had been a very happy man for most of his life. But in the latter years he

52

had developed a condition that had completely changed his personality. He had become very depressed, but also very angry and tearful in his last months.

Amanda had done all she could do make his last days comfortable. But her dad was highly irritable and could explode at any moment because of his change in personality. She admitted to me that this had driven her crazy at times.

When Ralph showed me an incident in which he sent a teacup full of scalding hot tea flying across the room, Amanda recognised it immediately.

She told me she had fled the room in floods of tears, unable to cope with this stranger in her home. She also admitted that she got very angry with him afterwards.

Ralph had known he wasn't his normal self in his last days. He showed me that at one point he had said to Amanda: 'I can't help who I am.'

'Yes, that's right,' she told me.

He knew how hard it was for Amanda and thanked her for the things she had done for him.

Amongst these were reuniting him with a close relative in Wales, from whom he'd become estranged. The key thing was that for a long time Amanda had been haunted by the thought that she had somehow let him down. She had felt guilty at the fact she had occasionally felt angry at him. And because of this she had been locked into an image of him in his final, difficult days.

There had clearly been a great deal of sadness in the family at Ralph's death. The weight of his passing had been heavy to bear for some.

Ralph told Amanda how pleased she was that she had poured her sister's antidepressants down the toilet.

As the communication drew to a close, I could sense that this had been an important message for Amanda. By communicating with the spirit of the father she had known all her life, not the man she had watched slip away from this life, she had been given the reassurance she needed to move on with her life.

From the smiles on her face as I gave her Ralph's best love and wishes, I could see that tonight, on the first anniversary of his passing, she was going to celebrate his life and his memory.

It is so easy for us to get caught up in the circumstances of someone's passing. Amanda, like so many of us, had allowed her memories of her father to be dominated by images and thoughts of his final days. She needed to sidestep the circumstances of his death and remember the jolly, kind-hearted man who had existed before his illness changed him.

On the first anniversary of his passing, I like to think I helped her achieve that.

Facing the Truth

The loss of someone important in your life can exaggerate and distort some of the feelings you had about them while they were alive. We are all guilty of this. For instance, some people have a great tendency to turn others into almost saintly beings in the immediate aftermath of their passing when, in truth, they were anything but. There is a great danger in putting people like this on pedestals.

Being completely honest with ourselves can be difficult, especially when we are having to accept some difficult truths. What if that person who has passed over wasn't a positive force in our life? What if, in fact, rather than being inspirational he or she had held us back in life? How do we move on from that? How do we acknowledge that?

I have encountered many people who have struggled to move on with their lives because they have failed to face up to the glaring truth about their real relationship with someone who has passed over. Often they are trapped by a mixture of guilt and fear.

I have, for instance, encountered people who have blamed themselves for the suicides of loved ones. They have carried the burden of these people's deaths with them for years. In such cases I invariably say the same thing: 'It wasn't your decision to leave this life, it was theirs. Nobody told them to do this, certainly not you.'

There is a natural tendency to speak in reverential terms about people who have recently passed over. The phrase 'don't speak ill of the dead' seems to exert a hold over all of us. It is, of course, common human decency to do so. But we also have to be realistic. There are times when we do need to speak, not necessarily ill of the dead, but at least honestly. We do need to face up to the truth that some people simply should not be put up on pedestals.

A Long Wait

I said at the beginning that this is not the sort of book that was going to provide you with a precise road map of the journey ahead. It could never be like that. Everyone is different. Everyone's experience is going to be different.

Some of you will understand the Message I have tried to convey in these pages even before finishing. You may have grasped it already. For others the meaning might still be taking shape in your mind. You may have to give yourself more time to absorb what I have said. You have to read certain sections—or even the whole book—again before you truly understand.

This is inevitable. Coming to terms with a subject as important as our connection to the afterlife isn't easy. It can also take a very long time for us to deal with a loss. Sometimes we don't even realise we are still grieving many, many years later.

I have encountered many people who have spent a long, long time grieving over someone who has passed over. In some cases, they didn't even realise they were doing so. One memorable reading springs to mind.

It happened at one of the most colourful venues where I've performed my live show, a place called the Circus Tavern in the East End of London.

The venue was a lively place to say the least. In the weeks prior to my appearing there, they had staged everything from live cage-fighting to pole dancing. The people who frequented the place were every bit as colourful. It was the sort of place where, if I'd started a message by saying I had someone coming through who had been stabbed or shot to death, about nine hundred hands would have gone up at the same time!

Appearing there was never anything less than an experience. And it certainly was an experience the night I got a message to a chap called Big Steve.

The type of people who connect through me

56

varies according to the venue, often. So it was no great surprise when one of the spirits I felt on this particular evening was a very big, tough-looking fellow. As he came through I felt sure he used to work at a circus.

'He's massive, this man. I can see him putting up a circus tent. I can see him knocking stakes into the ground and then hauling up this huge canvas,' I said.

Nobody reacted to this at first. All I could see in front of me was a sea of blank faces. But when I mentioned that I thought the spirit I had with me was trying to get into contact with someone called Big Steve, I couldn't help noticing the reaction of a very large and intimidating man at the bar.

'That's me,' he said, placing his pint glass down on the bar. This man was huge. He reminded me a little of the wrestler, Giant Haystacks. He had a mane of long, black hair and was well over six foot tall. He didn't look like someone to mess with.

I always say at the beginning of my shows that there are several types of people in the audience. There are those who believe absolutely in me and what I do and there are those who aren't sure but come along out of curiosity. And then there are the poor unfortunates, those that have been dragged along. This man clearly fitted into the latter category. Although who would have had the strength to drag him along was beyond me.

'Does the name Big Steve mean anything to you?'

'Yeah, people call me that,' he grunted, looking extremely suspiciously—and a little threateningly—at me.

'Does this person I'm describing sound familiar

to you?'

'Yeah, it does actually,' he replied. 'It sounds a lot like Dave, a kid I used to work with at a circus a long time ago.'

'Does the tent mean anything to you?'

'Yeah. Me and Dave used to put tents up together.'

I was reasonably confident now that I'd connected to the right person. I was soon a hundred per cent sure.

'He is showing me that he once sat on a nail,' I said. 'And it went right up his bottom.'

That produced gusts of laughter amongst most of the audience. Big Steve's reaction was somewhat different, however. He turned a ghostly white. For a moment I thought he was going to collapse in a heap on the floor.

'I have never told anyone that happened,' he said. 'Never.'

After that he started opening up to me a little. He said he was very good friends with Dave. 'We did some very dodgy things together when we were young,' he smiled at one point.

'Yes, I can see. He's showing me some of them,' I said, to his mild horror. 'Don't worry, I won't share them with the audience.'

Dave didn't have anything really important to pass on to Steve. 'The main thing he is telling me is that he misses all the fun you used to have together,' I said.

'Right,' Big Steve said, nodding.

'He says you were a good mate.'

'Thanks.'

After the show had ended I was surprised to find that Steve had hung back and was waiting to talk to

58

me. I was even more taken aback when, talking on our own in a corner of the club, he started crying.

'That man was like a brother to me,' he said. 'He died very young. It had a huge effect on me and I've never really talked about it to anyone. Hearing that tonight brought me back to that time and the adventures we used to have together.'

It turned out that Steve and Dave had worked at the circus when they were in their late teens. Steve was now into his forties. So it was more than twenty years since Dave had passed over.

'I guess I've been suppressing it all these years,' Steve told me.

Why his friend had come through that night remains a mystery to me. It was probably the first opportunity he would have had to make contact in the twenty years since he'd passed. As I say, I think Steve was dragged along to see me that night. I was pretty certain this was the first time he had come along to see a medium. What it did confirm to me, however, was the fact that people can postpone dealing with their feelings for very long periods. They can, like Steve, push their grief to one side and store it away for months, years, even decades.

The message Steve received that night was clearly a cathartic moment for him. And I was glad to have been able to deliver it to him. My only sadness was that he couldn't have crossed that bridge many years earlier. He would have rediscovered—and drawn strength from—his long lost friendship that much sooner.

Through the Eyes of a Child

If I had to sum up the one goal we should all set

ourselves in dealing with the loss of a loved one, it would be this: we all need to get to a point where we don't feel separation. Even though we have acknowledged that physically the person has passed on, we need to find a way to conduct our lives and carry on their memory that stimulates a closeness of a new and more spiritual kind.

If you learn to conduct your life without sorrow and a sense of loneliness and if you refuse to feel separated from loved ones then the barrier between the two dimensions can be as broad as an ocean or as thin as a hair.

There is, however, no set way of applying the ideas that I am going to outline in this book. Everyone is going to come up with their own, individual approach. Some of these approaches will be simple, some more complex.

During the course of my career, I've been moved by the way many people have responded to my ideas, but never more so than when I met a lady named Ruth. I met Ruth, not through my work as a medium, but at a seminar I gave on positive thinking.

When I first met her she was still in a quite severe state of grief. Her six-year-old daughter had died in terrible circumstances. She had slipped while playing in a paddling pool. Somehow she had banged her head on the side of the pool and been knocked unconscious. She had drowned in four inches of water.

To make matters even worse her daughter was staying with her grandparents at the time. So Ruth's grief was complicated by the fact she felt angry towards her parents and herself for leaving the child there.

When I met Ruth she was really suffering. She asked my advice on how she could get her life to move on. The answers I gave her were the same as the answers I will give you in this book.

I said, 'Well, first of all you have to acknowledge your daughter's life. You also have to sidestep the pain and acknowledge what her life has meant to you. You must then find a way of keeping her spirit close to you.'

I told her that it wouldn't be easy. I didn't mince my words. I was very blunt with her and said the fact that she had brought her daughter into the world, that she bathed her and washed her and changed her nappies and watched her grow up didn't mean that she owned her. And by the same token she didn't own her memory. So she couldn't become obsessive or possessive about her grief.

She had to move on, somehow keeping her daughter with her, in mind and spirit.

A couple of years later I met Ruth again. Once more it was at a seminar I was holding. The transformation in her was quite remarkable. Two years earlier she had been an emotional wreck. She had seemed so fragile you could have snapped her in half. Now she seemed, not strong exactly, but more at peace and certainly more confident in herself.

It was while talking to another student that I discovered how Ruth had achieved this. There was another woman called Sharon at the seminar who had experienced an eerily similar and tragic experience to Ruth. Sharon's daughter had drowned in a swimming pool. During a break in the course, I chatted to the two women.

At one point Sharon asked Ruth how she coped

with what had happened. 'How do you live with it?' she wondered.

'Well,' Ruth said, 'I've trained as a teacher's assistant. I now work at a school.'

This produced a shocked reaction in Sharon. Her expression looked as if to say: *How could you torture yourself like that*? She seemed incredulous.

Ruth read her face and answered the unspoken question. 'I said to myself: "If I can't have my daughter then I will see something of her in every other child I work with,"' she explained. 'So now in the eyes of every happy child I see my daughter. Every time I see a child playing I look into their eyes and see my daughter. That's how I live with it.'

Sharon was moved to tears by this, as was I. 'You are very brave,' she eventually said to Ruth.

Ruth just smiled warmly and shook her head. 'No, I'm not brave,' she said. 'It's simply that this is the only way I can remain close to my daughter.'

I was extremely moved by her story. It remains one of the most poetic personal stories I have ever heard and I think it is one from which we can all learn a great deal.

PART TWO

Harmony

You must eliminate fear in the same way that your loved ones have done on the other side.

A World Without Fear

People are understandably curious about what it must be like to be a medium. It is, I suppose, an unusual way to live your life, even though it seems perfectly normal to me.

One of the most common questions I'm asked is whether I can ever switch off. 'How do you ever get to sleep at nights?' someone asked me recently, a slightly concerned look on her face.

I find it interesting that people would even ask this question. It reveals, I think, the huge misconception that many now have about the spirit world. People seem to have the idea that it is jam-packed full of lost, damaged and slightly scary souls.

Part of this, I think, is down to the success of some of the most popular 'ghost-hunter'-style television programmes. I don't have a problem with shows like *Most Haunted*. They are good entertainment. But I do think they have created the false idea that the world is full of tortured souls wandering around in search of redemption.

This is simply not my experience of the afterlife. And it is why I sleep easily—and well—most nights. The truth is that when the overwhelming majority of us end our earthly lives we pass over into the spirit world immediately. We don't hang around in a limbo, somewhere between the two dimensions. We pass over, usually after a period of transition.

What I see when I glimpse the spirit world is a place full of light, energy and brightness. It is a place without conflict. It is a happy place.

So, for me, it is not something that keeps me awake at night. Far from it, there is nothing negative or scary about the other side at all. Truth be told, I don't really understand why anyone would be frightened by the dead. All that has changed is that the person you knew before has moved on into the parallel world. Were you scared of that person during their earthly existence? If not, why would you be scared of them now? It makes no sense. They are still the same person. You can still interact with them if you give them the chance.

I long for the day when everyone accepts the eternity of the soul, that we are all eternal and we all carry on. There would be no need for mediums at all then. And then I would get a really good night's sleep. But for now, that is a distant prospect.

*   *   *

There are many misconceptions about the afterlife and it is my job to correct as many of them as possible and to answer as many questions as possible.

One of the subtler and more interesting questions I am asked every now and again, is this: if the parallel world is so full of the spirits of those who have passed over, how does it exist without conflict? How can it be so peaceful over there? This is actually a very good question, because it also opens up something that applies here in our earthly existence. The answer boils down to one word: fear.

The reason the spirit world exists without all the

negative aspects that plague the earthly plane is that there is no fear there. Those who exist there are living unafraid of the things that make life here in this existence sometimes difficult.

To move on with our lives after someone's passing so that we can re-connect with them in the spirit world, we must eliminate fear in the same way as they have done on the other side.

So, as we move on, having spent some time focusing on that which has gone, the person we have lost, we must now spend some time thinking about ourselves. And as we do so, we must eliminate our fear.

Making Peace with Yourself

If you want to understand the Message, if you want to feel that closeness to the spirit of those who have passed over, then you must be happy with yourself. You must be at peace with who you are.

We all need to find harmony, balance or equilibrium in our life. If you don't feel harmonious about who you are, if you are filled with fear, anger, regret, resentment, self-doubt or any other negative feeling, then you are not going to reach a point where you are going to feel close to the spirit side.

It is, in a way, like putting your foot on a hosepipe. The spirit world may be ready to flow in your direction, but because you are blocking its route, it cannot come through. Or put it another way. It is like a padlock on a box. Inside the box is the knowledge and understanding that will change your life. But you are never going to have it revealed to you when, actually, you don't like yourself very much.

You can't have balance until you've eliminated that which is unnecessary. It's really about turfing out the emotional clutter.

It is therefore vital that during this part of the process you start to eliminate your regrets, your doubts, your inadequacy, or sense of inadequacy. You must jettison these negative things for good and consign them to the past. Until you do so life isn't going to move on.

*   *   *

I'd like to share with you a story about a lady who, rather neatly, sums up the lack of harmony that can inhibit a person who is trying to move on with their life.

I first saw this middle-aged lady as she stood patiently in line while I was doing a book signing at the end of an evening show in the Midlands. When her turn came, Rita smiled a little nervously. 'Hello, Colin. I enjoyed the show very much, but I had been hoping that my mum would come through,' she confessed.

This, of course, is something that I encounter all the time. I have no idea which members of the audience are going to be related to the spirits with which I am going to make a connection. So, inevitably, in every audience there are always some people who are slightly disappointed that it was not them who received the communication. It is simply the way it is. I am not going to be able to get a connection for each and every member of a 2,000 or 3,000 strong audience.

But there was something about this woman. I

had a feeling I should help her. So I made an exception to my normal rule and said I would see her again on my own. 'Don't tell me anything more now. I will see you privately,' I said.

We set up an appointment and she came to see me a short time later. I was able to make a connection with her mother, who had passed away within the past year or so. What she had to say made an immediate impact.

'I've got your mother here and she is showing me that she was in a nursing home environment before she passed over,' I said.

'Yes, that's right,' Rita agreed.

'She wants you to know that you were quite correct,' I said. 'Do you understand what that might mean?'

'Yes,' she said, looking quite shaken. 'I think I do understand what that might mean.'

'Your mother is telling me that she wants you to know that you shouldn't have any problems any more about that.'

The effect this had on Rita was quite powerful. After I'd ended the communication with her mother, she became very emotional and began telling me what had happened.

Her mother had been afflicted by Alzheimer's, a terrible illness that devastates the lives of many families. As her mother had become less and less aware of her surroundings, Rita and her sister had put her into a safe environment, in a home for the last stage of her life.

Alzheimer's is a cruel condition. I have made connections with many who suffered from its ravages, usually with their faculties restored on the other side. As the disease had developed and her mother's mental state deteriorated, Rita had found it simply too harrowing to watch. She agonised about it for a long time but eventually she made the decision and she had stopped visiting her.

'I felt terribly guilty about it but I couldn't bear to be near her towards the end,' she told me. 'The woman I was seeing wasn't my mother any more. It was her body but she wasn't there and I couldn't stand it. As far as I was concerned my mother was dead a long time before she actually died.'

This had caused enormous friction with her sister. She became very angry with her because she felt Rita had abandoned their mother. It caused huge damage to their relationship. The anger her sister felt at her had endured long after their mother's passing. Before their mother's death they had been very close. Afterwards, however, there was a lasting rift between them.

As we talked, I shared some thoughts with Rita.

To begin with, I told her that she had done all she could. She had put her mother in a safe environment. She had entrusted her to professionals who were there to provide the twenty-four-hour care she needed.

What more could she have done?

Secondly, I reassured her that she had done what she felt was right.

Often people's disharmony after someone passes over stems from that fact that family, friends and society have punished them for how they have dealt with the situation. 'Many people might think what you did was awful. Many people might be judgmental and say "How could you do that to your mother?"' I told her. 'But you did what you thought was right. And that was all you could do.

'You paid the bills, you phoned once a week and asked the matron whether she was comfortable,' I said. 'Your mother's dementia was so bad she wasn't asking for you. If you'd seen her she probably wouldn't have known who the hell you were.

'Your sister chose to do something different and continued to visit. She chose to go through the agony of seeing this woman who she loved, staring blankly at her without any acknowledgement at all. That was her decision. Not yours. She did what she thought was right. So did you.'

As she left me I could almost see the burden lifting off Rita's shoulders. I felt sure that she was going to be able to get on with her life, no longer weighed down by the guilt that had been holding her back.

Rita's predicament was, of course, far from unique. An awful lot of people use this expression: 'Well, you know—if only I'd done more for them.'

You have to sit down and work that one through by yourself: what more could you have done?

I remember a conversation I had with one woman who felt deeply that she could have done more to help her mother deal with the pain she had suffered during her final days. 'I should have helped more with her pain,' she kept saying to me.

I just shook my head and asked her a simple question. 'Did you ask the doctors to give her medication?'

'Yes, I did,' she nodded.

'Did you ask them whether there was anything more they could do to help ease her pain?'

'Yes. I did.'

'So what more do you think you could personally have done that would have prevented her pain? What were you going to do? Invent a new drug? Find a new medical cure? Be realistic. There wasn't anything more you could have done for her.'

As you look for harmony, the important thing is that you accept the reality of the situation. What did you have it in your power to achieve? What realistically could you have done?

Finding Your Path

I can't stress enough how important it is that we understand that our relationship with those who have passed over is a dynamic one. It goes on. It evolves beyond death.

As we look for the peace and harmony we need in order to get on with our earthly existence, we sometimes have to address and change these relationships.

As we move on in the weeks, months and years that follow bereavement, we need to be clear about the direction we take. We need to be sure of what we are doing—and why we are doing it. At this stage, we must watch out for the effects of what I call 'negative grief'. People who display negative grief are more concerned with pleasing the person who has passed over than they are in caring for themselves.

There is, of course, nothing wrong with choosing a path in life that is inspired by the example of the person who has passed over. Far from it, this can be the key to successfully keeping both your own life and the spirit of your loved one fresh and alive.

But there is a big difference between that and doing things to please those who have passed over out of guilt or, even worse, fear.

I have encountered many people who feel that because they were never able to fulfil a person's expectations of them in life they must continue to try to win their approval after their death. They think to themselves: 'Now that that person has passed over I must try to do things to win their approval or be that person they wanted me to be because I failed to do that in life.'

A few years ago, I did a reading for Cathy, a lady who worked as a nurse at a local hospital. I suspect she was a very good nurse as well.

But as I sat with Cathy I could feel a general dissatisfaction with her lot in life during the reading. 'I sense you hate your job,' I said to her at one point.

'Yes, I do,' she replied.

The person who came through to her during the reading was her mother. As I connected with her, the roots of her daughter's unhappiness became clear. 'Your mother is showing me that it was her who wanted you to be a nurse,' I said. 'It wasn't you.'

'No,' she said.

'You were thinking of giving it up during your nurses' training course because you hated it. You knew you couldn't spend the rest of your life doing this job,' I said.

'Yes.' Cathy nodded again.

'It was your mother who kept telling you you had to carry on.'

'That's right.'

As the reading went on it transpired that her

mother had died while Cathy was still training. It had been a terrible time for Cathy. Her grief had been mixed up with an awful jumble of conflicting emotions. She hated her job more than ever. Every day required a huge effort for her to put on her uniform. She wanted to quit her course more than ever. But her mother's presence now loomed even larger than it had during life. It hung over her telling her that she couldn't walk away, she had to finish what she had started.

So she continued training and qualified as a nurse. But she did so for her mum, not for herself.

Of course, in some circumstances you could have argued that her mother had done her a positive service. You could have concluded that she knew best and dismissed her daughter's desire to quit as some form of childish rebellion against her domineering influence. But it wasn't that. Cathy had genuinely taken a wrong turn in life. She had gone down a path that had made her genuinely unhappy and was, frankly, ruining her life. The acid test was that it was now six years since her mother's passing and she still absolutely hated her job.

But she continued to do it because she thought that's what her mother wanted her to do.

This kind of negative grief is almost as bad as the person who refuses to ever draw back their curtains or who walks around telling everyone that their life is over. It is destructive and wrong.

I decided I had to try to act on it.

I never usually ask people questions during my readings but in this case I did. 'If your mum was still here would you give up nursing?' I wondered.

Cathy's response was instant. 'Oh yes, I'd have

told her. We'd have had a big argument about it, but I would have done it. That's what's so frustrating. I just can't let her down now.'

'That's not true,' I said. 'You're letting her down by continuing to do a job you hate. Tell her now.'

'What?' she said.

'Tell her now. Say: "Look, Mum, I can't follow this path. It was always your dream, it was never my dream."'

Cathy sat looking at me for a moment. Then, together, we told her mother that she was going to resign from her job that week.

I sensed her mother didn't like it. But she accepted it.

*   *   *

We can still re-establish the boundaries of our relationship with people after their passing in this way. At times it is a necessity if we are ever to find the peace and harmony we need in this life.

None of us should do things simply to please people on the other side any more than we would if they were on this side of life. If, deep down, it makes us so unhappy that our lives here are ruined as a result, we must simply say no. This is especially the case in instances where people have been overpowering and domineering influences.

This is, of course, something you need to do during your act of acknowledgement. You must ask yourself whether you were pushed around and bullied by that person? And if you find they were domineering in life are you going to allow them to remain domineering on the other side? Or is this where you are going change the boundaries.

Sometimes it is a question of sitting down and having a conversation. You may need to say: 'Look, Mum (or Dad), you always expected me to do what you wanted, but now this is my time. This is where I'm going to change my life. I've spent my entire life trying to please you. I love you and I want to feel connected to you. But I want to tell you that from now on I am going to live my life the way that I want it to be.'

This is exactly what happened when I met a young lady called Helen a few years ago. The domineering force she was faced with was her grandmother.

When Helen arrived at my home for a reading my heart sank at first. I used to dread young people coming to see me because so many had the wrong idea about what I do. To avoid wasting my and their time, I learned to ask them in advance whether they had a clear idea about why they were seeing me.

When I asked Helen she replied immediately: 'Oh, yes. I'm here about the man I'm about to marry.'

This made me feel even more despondent. 'Oh no, here we go again,' I thought to myself. 'This is going to be a psychic reading. She wants to know if she is marrying the right man.'

I used to hate readings like that. The people who came along for them were never interested in the mediumship side of what I do. In effect, they wanted a bit of fortune telling, which I don't do.

So my expectations were low as I began. However, I soon changed my opinion of Helen as my mind became flooded with a series of images. 'You were raised by your grandmother, weren't

75

you?' I said to Helen.

'Yes, that's right,' she confirmed.

'I have her here with me. I know your mum and dad are still alive and your grandmother isn't showing me the exact circumstances, but you actually lived with her.'

'Yes,' she said.

As the reading intensified I saw that the grandmother had exerted a very strong influence over Helen throughout her life. Perhaps too strong an influence, I sensed already.

Helen looked as though she was in her late teens or early twenties. She was a pretty girl and had got a boyfriend. I could feel that the grandmother didn't approve of him. It was more than a dislike actually, it was a hatred. She absolutely hated him.

As her grandmother got older and more crotchety, it got to the point where she forbade Helen's boyfriend to even set foot anywhere near the house. When Helen went out with him in the evening she had to meet him at the gate.

Despite her grandmother's protestations, Helen had not just carried on seeing her boyfriend, she had got engaged to him. This, needless to say, had made her grandmother even angrier. Which was why she did what she did towards the very end of her life.

In the week she was dying, the grandmother made Helen promise not to marry this man. By that time, not only were the couple engaged, they had set a wedding day and even started to make the arrangements for the big day.

Helen had come to me in the hope that her grandmother was going to back down and let her go ahead.

I could sense very quickly that wasn't going to happen. However, I also sensed that I had to talk some sense into Helen before she made a big mistake. Relationships continue to change beyond the boundaries of death. And we have to be honest about the nature of those relationships. We have to ask whether it was always a productive relationship. Was it always a positive one? If the answer is no, then the dynamic of this relationship has to change, even when the people involved are separated. I sensed this was what needed to happen here. Helen had to stand up to her grandmother in the next life, in a way she hadn't done while she was in this life.

I told her, 'You have got to get the message across to Grandma and say, "This is my life and if you were physically here I would have told you to your face. Sorry you can't decide for me who I can and can't marry. You may have your reservations about him and you might even be right, but nonetheless it's my choice. You don't have the right to rule my life."'

During our reading Helen asked me to pass this message on to her grandmother, which I did. To my relief I heard a few weeks later that Helen had gone ahead and got married.

I'm utterly convinced that if I hadn't seen her, she would have cancelled her wedding purely because her grandma had made this dying wish. Fortunately she'd now had an opportunity to take a long, hard look at her relationship with her grandmother and she had seen the light.

As we can see from these two last examples, someone's passing over can actually mark a really good time for us to make positive changes by becoming truer to who we really are. We can't turn ourselves into someone we are not. But we can certainly turn ourselves into someone closer to the person that we aspire to be. We can find a harmony and an inner peace that has, perhaps, been missing since long before our bereavement began.

The Negative Buck Stops Here

As we deal with the passing of someone important we are approaching an important crossroads in our lives. We will soon be facing important choices about the direction our life is going to take from now on. So it is vitally important that we are harmonious about everything that has happened in our lives so far. And we are not just talking about dealing with the person who has passed over. This is a chance to deal with every experience, every relationship, every person that has made an impact on our existence so far.

How will we know that we have achieved this? What do we need to have done to get to this point? Everyone is going to have to make peace with themselves in their own way, of course. We all have issues in our past, people in our lives, that we need to think about and deal with. But we should all be asking ourselves questions like:

- Are we harmonious not just with the person who has recently passed over, but with everyone we know who has left this earthly plane? If not, can we now see how to make our peace with them?
- Have we really forgiven everybody in our lives who has ever hurt us? If not, can we now seek to forgive them either directly or

through our actions?
- Have we forgiven ourselves for every hurt that we've caused others in our lives?
- If we have damaged people have we acknowledged that damage?
- Are we happy that we have dealt with the key moments in our lives in the right way? If we aren't, are we resolved that if we are ever in that situation again we will handle it differently?

By dealing with all these issues we can all give ourselves a really clear vision of a happier and more peaceful future.

None of this is easy, of course. As I know only too well from my own life. I've had many experiences in my life, some good, many bad and an awful lot indifferent. But I don't think that I would be the medium or the person I am or be able to do the things I do had I not had those experiences. They have brought me a kind of harmony.

I have had to acknowledge the wrongs I have done to others and I have had to acknowledge the wrongs that have been done to me. And I have had to forgive. But I have also had to learn how to do so. Let me give you one, small example.

I often get asked about evil spirits. Do they exist in the spirit world? Do I encounter them during readings? My answer is always the same. I have encountered the hurt and the damaged, the frightened and the angry. Just as I have in this earthly life. But that doesn't make them evil.

Whenever I encounter a hurt or damaged spirit I always consider what was done to them to make them this way. It is the same in this life. There are people in life who have gone out of the way to deliberately hurt me. I used to resent them for it. Now I think, 'Who has done this to you?' Now I know their behaviour is invariably a result of something that has been done to them.

A while ago I was walking through the town of Burgess Hill, near where I grew up. At the time my television show *6ixth Sense* was starting its second series and was becoming very popular.

As I was walking along the High Street I saw a guy who had been at school with me. My memories of him were far from happy. As a child I had been very small and this guy used to bully me.

I had seen the guy around over the years. I have to say that at this point I don't think I had ever forgiven him for the way he had treated me.

To my surprise he started walking towards me. 'Oh, hi, Colin,' he said. 'My wife's a huge fan of yours. Could you sign an autograph for her?'

I just said, 'I don't do autographs,' and walked away.

It was, I know, a childish thing to do, but actually, for a fleeting moment, I felt a bit of one-upmanship. The satisfaction was very short lived, however. By the time I got home I felt pretty stupid. I thought to myself: 'That was a pretty petty thing to do.'

A few months later I was walking through Burgess Hill again and I saw the same guy. I could tell immediately that he wasn't going to approach me again so this time I went up to him. 'Look, I'm really sorry about what happened a couple of months ago. Do you still want an autograph for your wife?' I asked.

'Oh, yes, thanks, Colin. That would be great,' he replied.

As I was signing he looked at me. 'I'm really sorry for what I did to you when we were kids,' he said. 'But I'm not the same person any more.'

And I looked at him and said: 'No, and neither am I. So why don't we just forget about it?'

We shook hands and walked away.

I went home that day feeling an awful lot better. As I analysed my feelings I realised it was because he had asked me to forgive him. I felt good about the fact that it was within my power to do so.

The experience proved a real learning curve for me. I discovered subsequently that this guy's father was a drunken brute who used to knock the hell out of him when he was young. A child who is treated like that at home is either going to become very withdrawn or they are going to strike out and inflict the same thing on someone else. That's what he had done.

When we were at school he used to call me names, intimidate me, hit me. It was a horrible time for me. When I'd seen him in the street that first time it was almost as if I wanted to slap him back for all the times he'd slapped me.

I was glad that I'd had the opportunity to see the bigger picture.

It is very easy for people to say bullies are cowards. It goes deeper than that. Why does a bully pick on people who are smaller than them? You have to ask: What was done to them?

It's something we can all take on board. Think of when you last behaved badly towards somebody. If you look at what was happening at the time, I'm prepared to bet that you were taking out on them something that has been done to you.

Sometimes you have to look at a situation and think, *I have to forgive everyone who has hurt me. So that I can be forgiven for how I passed that on to other people.*

This is the sort of thinking that we all need to practise as we go through the process of finding harmony and peace in our lives. You can pass on the positive things. But you can also decide that anything negative ends with you. You can decide that you will deal with it.

I could write a book about harmony and its importance. But for now, you need to write the next chapters of that book for yourself.

PART THREE

Re-emergence

You can reach a point where you can say: bereavement has made me a stronger and even a better person.

From Weakness to Strength

As the philosopher Friedrich Nietzsche wrote, 'What doesn't kill us makes us stronger.' Bereavement is a weakening experience. Having someone we love pass over drains us of our energy and our positive energy in particular. This creates a barrier between us and the spirit world. This in turn means that we remain separated from the new existence that our loved ones are experiencing there.

If we are to restore that connection we must restore ourselves. We must move on with our lives and to do that we need to renew our positive energy.

I am passionate about the power of positive thinking. I strongly believe that, by approaching life in the right way, we can all reach a point where we can say: 'Bereavement has made me a stronger and even a better person.' The best way to do that is by putting the past behind us and turning the things that have been our weaknesses into our strengths.

To begin that process we must re-enter the world. We must draw back the curtains that we closed when the person we loved passed over. We must let the world back in and say goodbye to that period where we have been looking out of the window watching life go by. It is the time when we brace ourselves to rejoin it and say to ourselves I want to be part of that.

Good Vibrations

You cannot change the past. It has happened. You can only come to terms with the past. You come to terms with who that person was. What their impact on your life has been. You can harmonise all those events and relationships in your life, what that person did or didn't mean to you, your regrets, your failures, your achievements.

Once you've achieved that, you need to begin the next stage in the process. You must now deal with the present. You must face up to your life in the here and now.

To begin this process, however, you must first step out of yourself and back into the wider world. And to do that, you must be ready to give yourself to that world. Unfortunately, this isn't always easy. In fact, for many people, it is one of the hardest things they have to do.

I always begin my live shows by asking people to do two things, the first of which is simply to smile. I don't just do this so that I have a theatre full of happy faces staring at me. There is a more serious reason.

Spirits exist in a lighter, brighter, faster plane. They need an environment that reflects this. So they are not going to come through on what I call a vibration of misery. If the people they are trying to contact are too sombre or sad or dark the atmosphere is too dense. Communications get lost or they don't get through at all.

Trying to have positive thoughts can be a challenge, of course, especially when many people

85

have come along bearing thoughts of loved ones who they miss very much. Many people come along to see me with their minds still full of the sad and unhappy times they associate with the person's passing. So I ask people in my audiences to put these out of their minds and focus on happy memories. I also encourage those who aren't going to receive messages during the evening to feel happy for those who do. If the lady sitting a few rows away from them gets a message telling her that her mother is well in the spirit world, then they too should feel that their mother is in a good place. It is amazing how energising this positive thinking can be.

Next, I ask people not to sit with their arms crossed. There are two very simple reasons for this. One, it is a very defensive signal. By sitting there with their arms locked they are putting up barriers that will almost certainly guarantee that no communication is going to occur. Two, the human body has a number of energy centres, one of which is the solar plexus region in the lower region of your chest. By blocking this area you are impeding a very particular energy, one that is associated with giving. By folding your arms you are signalling that you are not prepared to give. And if you don't give then you won't receive.

The same principle applies when you are getting ready to re-enter the wider world. As the story of a lady I worked with many years ago illustrates.

*   *   *

One afternoon a few years ago a lady came to me for a reading. Nothing unusual about this, of course. I have conducted thousands of readings in the thirty years I have been a practising medium.

There was something that made this woman stand out from all the others I'd sat with during those three decades, however. She was probably the saddest-looking person that I'd ever met. You only had to look at the rims around her eyes to know that she probably spent three quarters of her life crying. She had probably kept Kleenex in profit single-handedly.

I wasn't altogether surprised when the reading proved a failure. As I sat there with her she gave out nothing but negative energy. As I tell my audiences time and time again, if you don't give you don't receive. And so it proved again here. Nothing happened.

I used to have a rule if you come to me three times and nothing happens then I'm probably not the right medium for you. This lady came back twice more and, as before, nothing happened.

But there was something about her that made me feel I should persevere. Her sadness seemed so deep I wanted to do the best I could to try to lift it. So I saw her about seven times during the course of the next six months.

The world of mediumship is small and we all know each other well. So I knew that she was seeing other mediums and they were having exactly the same results with her. They were getting nothing too. They too were conducting readings in which this lady would sit there for an hour waiting forlornly for something to come through.

But then something unexpected happened.

I was getting ready to meet her again one day. To be honest, I was quietly dreading her visit. I was bracing myself to tell her that there really was no point in me seeing her again.

When she arrived, however, she looked different. She was ever-so-slightly more cheerful. It wasn't a huge transformation. She still wasn't exactly radiating the joys of spring. But she was definitely a lighter, happier presence than she'd been before.

It was just enough. Suddenly everything happened. During what was meant to be her final session, all sorts of spirits came through. There were friends, relatives and—most importantly—her husband.

Whereas normally I would do a sitting for an hour, this went on for nearly two hours. All sorts of information came through and as this was going on the lady was getting brighter and brighter. It was as if the lights had been out inside her and someone had tripped the switch to bring them on again.

Eventually, with me close to exhaustion, the reading drew to a close. But as he was about to break the connection with me, her husband had one final message for his wife.

'He is saying, "I'm sorry it's taken me so long to get through to you,"' I said. '"But you didn't give me anything to talk to you about."'

I don't think I have ever passed on a simpler message that resonated so strongly not just for this woman but for so many people who I see.

Chatting afterwards, the lady was in buoyant mood. So I asked her what it was that she had done differently from the last time I'd seen her.

'My daughter persuaded me to go out with her and the grandchildren for the day,' she said. 'I actually felt quite guilty because I quite enjoyed myself.'

I smiled. She had done the one thing that she desperately needed to do. Until now she'd been avoiding her family, not wanting to see anybody, coming to me hoping that I would give her the connection she wanted, and nothing had happened. She had taken one small step out into the world and that had changed everything for her, almost immediately.

'Why are you smiling?' she wondered.

'Don't you realise? That was the catalyst, that's what you needed to do to make it possible for your husband to come through to you,' I told her. 'You've been coming to me for all these months, coming from behind your closed curtains and closed door. You just needed to draw back those curtains.'

This is what we all need to do if we are to overcome our grief and re-connect not just with the earthly world, but with the loved ones who have passed over to the spirit world. We all need to draw back the curtains, we all need to let the world—or worlds—back in.

When you think about it, I'm sure it makes perfect sense. If we return from the funeral service then draw the curtains on our lives, telling ourselves that our life has ended in the same way that we believe the life of our loved one has ended, then we must expect to have to bear the consequences.

We can't in the next breath say: 'I am withdrawing from this world until I get some sign from them, until they tell me that they are still part of my life.' That's simply not going to happen.

Apart from anything else, what are they going to

talk to you about? What are they going to say to you? It will probably be something along the lines of: 'Hello, I'm living this wonderful bright sunny existence in my new world and I'm looking at you sitting in a darkened room with the curtains drawn, crying your eyes out all the time. And you wonder why I don't communicate with you.'

I know it may sound harsh but this is an important message for us all to understand. It applies wherever we are. Sending out a negative or closed vibration is simply not encouraging any kind of connection with the spirit world. If we want to keep them close, if we want to feel them around us, we need to send out good vibrations.

Arm Yourself with Experience

As we know, we cannot change the past. What we can do, however, is draw on the experiences of that past and use them to our advantage in the future. We can turn what were our weaknesses into our strengths. We can make our experiences of pain our armour.

As we re-connect with the world, there is going to be no shortage of situations where we will get an opportunity to do this. There are going to be reminders of the person who has passed over everywhere we go, whether it is to the supermarket or the cinema, to church or to school in the mornings. It is inevitable. We will not be able to escape it. So we must begin to face up to the prospect of dealing with it.

Some of these encounters are going to stimulate more powerful emotions than others, of course. How are we going to deal with the first funeral we have to attend after we've lost a loved one? How are we going to draw on the experience we have been through there? We have to be prepared to deal with each of them, however.

Let's look at an example. What if someone else we know suffers a bereavement? Perhaps a friend loses her husband in the same way that we have just done. When that happens, we have a choice. We can let it open the floodgates and bring back all the memories of our own recent grieving. We can think to ourselves: 'I have barely recovered from my husband's funeral. How can I possibly go to this one? It will be too much.'

Or we can use it as a positive. We can see an opportunity to go along and use our own experience of pain and bereavement to help someone else through it. This is going to help us too because it will give us a sense of perspective. We can go along in the knowledge we are not the only person that is going through this. Now somebody else is going through it as well.

Another example: let's say our child has died in infancy or we have suffered a miscarriage during pregnancy. What if a sister or brother announces they are expecting a child? How are you going to draw on the memories that you have of your own loved one? How are you going to draw on the pain that you went through when you had to bury your own loved one? What reserves of strength are you going to draw upon?

You are either going to go totally to pieces and think this is not fair. How on earth am I supposed to deal with this? How can life be so cruel? How can they be experiencing such happiness when I am feeling nothing but sorrow?

Or you can embrace a wonderful opportunity to rejoice, to celebrate what was good about the fact that, not long ago, you too were pregnant. Now somebody else is having the opportunity to have a child. You could feel happy for them.

This is something I have experienced recently. In the space of a very short time, I had three close friends who lost their babies. Two miscarried and the other was advised to have a termination because she was carrying a severely disabled child. These were terribly sad times, they were all desperate for a child.

I tend to be someone people turn to at these times and they each came to me asking for comfort. I simply told each of them it just wasn't meant to be on this occasion. The two who had miscarried took this well enough. The other one, however, was inconsolable. She felt it was so unfair. She had carried her child for months, only to see its life cut short. For a while she railed against the world for denying her something she wanted so badly. She couldn't talk about it without welling up. She couldn't bear to look at a young mother walking down the street with a baby in a buggy. It would send her diving for cover in floods of tears.

So I asked her to begin turning this weakness into a strength. I asked her to imagine that her baby had gone full term and been born with the severe disability the doctors had diagnosed. She would have had to devote so many years of her life to coping with a mentally or physically handicapped child. Now, I knew she would have been willing to face that challenge. But the best medical advice had been to terminate.

The key thing was that she was still relatively young. There had been no particular problems with her health during the pregnancy. After the termination the doctors said she was still capable of having more children. They also said the chances of her having a normal, healthy child next time were pretty good.

'Don't you think that God, the universe, nature, whatever you want to call it, made the right decision,' I said to her. 'Don't you think this was just not meant to be? This was one that wasn't meant to come into the world. You will have another child, you know that.'

She shook her head. 'Why do I have to go through this pain?' she asked me.

My answer to that was simple. 'Because by experiencing that pain it is going to make you an even better parent. You are going to be a stronger mother,' I told her. 'This is the way that you have to start thinking.'

Less than a year later, she fell pregnant again. This time the pregnancy went full term with no complications. She and her husband now have a wonderful child.

Life is going to present you with many difficult moments. Every now and again, it is going to slap you in the face with things that appear to be unfair. But when it does so it is also going to give you the most amazing opportunities to rejoice. And if you are able to do that you are achieving something significant. You are allowing your negative experience to become a source of positive energy. You are turning that weakness into your strength.

This is also the point at which we tell ourselves we will never repeat any of the negative or unhelpful things that were said to us when we were grieving. We will think carefully before saying the kind of things that deepened rather than diminished our own pain.

We will never say: 'Get over it.' Or, 'Get a grip of yourself.' We won't say stupid things like, 'You're still young enough to find another husband.' Or, 'There's plenty of time for another baby.'

As shown by the story of another young mother I met recently, we will resolve never to act as insensitively as others do to us.

I saw this young woman jumping out of the car that had pulled up outside my house. She was youngish, in her early to mid-twenties, and as she shut the door behind her and waved to the man sitting in the driver's seat, she seemed to be in a highly agitated state.

'Are you OK?' I said as I sat her down with a cup of coffee a few minutes later.

'Fine,' she said, rather unconvincingly.

A medium cannot ever guarantee any response from the spirit world. Just like transatlantic phone calls in the days before satellites, there are times when the lines of communication are as clear as a bell and there are times when all you can hear is the distant hiss of static. So I began as I normally do by explaining this.

'I may get something but I may not get something,' I said. 'But if I don't there's nothing ominous about it. It just means a connection wasn't meant to take place.'

I say this to everyone, but I could see that the thought of her coming along and nothing happening was disturbing her.

I don't often get nervous before doing a reading but in this case I felt the lady's jitteriness was affecting me. 'Please let something happen, please,' I kept saying to myself.

Fortunately soon after we began I sensed a woman there, it was her grandmother. I said, 'I've got a lady here who is your grandmother. I know you don't have an Irish accent yourself but I can tell you have an Irish family.'

'Yes, that's right,' she said.

The connection with the grandmother was strong and very quickly I was getting a lot from her. 'She has a baby in her arms. A little boy. I wanted at first to say that he had never been born but I can see I'm wrong now. Your grandmother is showing me that he did live but for only a very short period of time,' I said. 'I am seeing fourteen days.'

'Yes,' she nodded.

What happened next was something I will never forget. 'Your grandmother is telling me that the priest is wrong,' I said. 'And the fact that she has the baby in her arms is evidence that the priest was wrong. Do you understand that?'

The moment the words passed my lips the woman just erupted into tears. I think I gave her an entire box of Kleenex. As she dabbed away at her running mascara, she kept saying 'thank you'. As the lady's mood lightened so too did the vibration I was getting from her grandmother.

I always tell people not to ask me anything specific, but she couldn't help it. 'Has she told the baby's name?' she asked.

'Yes, she has,' I smiled. 'And it's funny because he had exactly the same name as my stepbrother

Michael. The baby's name is Michael Patrick. Michael after your father and Patrick after your partner's father.'

That was it as far as she was concerned. Almost immediately she relaxed and sat back as if there was nothing more she needed or wanted to know. 'You've said everything I needed to hear today,' she said when I brought the reading to an end. 'My husband is going to be so pleased. He's sitting out in the car because he was too afraid to come in.'

We spent a few minutes talking afterwards and it was then that she explained to me what had happened to her.

She told me that her baby had died at fourteen days of age. He had never left the hospital. He had been born prematurely and never got out of the incubator. They thought he was going to be fine but then he got a lung infection and faded and passed in a matter of a few hours.

She came from a Catholic family, so they had contacted a priest and organised a Catholic funeral. The funeral took place and afterwards the elderly priest came up to her and said: 'I have to tell you, dear, that your baby can't really go to heaven because it wasn't baptised.' He added, 'God's got a special place for those lost babies.'

And it just devastated her.

She thought: 'My baby hasn't gone to heaven.'

She was only a young girl. She was clever but she was indoctrinated into the Catholic faith. When she came to me she said: 'I'm not supposed to see someone like you.'

'I know,' I said.

'But I couldn't believe that my baby had just gone into nothing,' she told me.

I am not knocking religion but this one case made my blood boil. I was outraged at what I'd heard. I thought a priest was supposed to be there to comfort his congregation. How could he tell someone something like that in this day and age?

He said completely the wrong thing. He is someone who is supposed to be spiritually guiding his congregation towards his vision of God and love.

Thankfully the communication I had with her grandmother was able to give her the information that she needed. As I watched her go I felt certain that she was going to go out and use the experience in a positive way.

I felt sure that she was going to take her pain, take her weakness and turn it into a strength from then on. Hopefully, she would feel strong enough to go out and say, *I know my baby survived. And I have evidence he survived.* She can tell those others who are told their babies haven't gone to heaven: *I have evidence that it's not true.*

What that priest had told her might have scarred her for life. Not only had nature taken away her baby, it had taken away her faith.

This sitting helped her find her faith again. But it also allowed her to transform something that had been causing her pain into something she could use positively in the future. She had transformed a weakness into a strength.

Don't Become Obsessed

If you analyse any human relationship, you see that it is a dynamic thing. Nothing stays the same. It changes on a day-to-day, even a minute-to-minute

97

basis. Each new sentence, thought and experience that you share with your husband, wife, partner or friend changes the dynamics of that relationship.

There are ups and downs, of course. There can't be very many human relationships where one partner is pleased with the other person all the time. We have a mixture of experiences, but that's what keeps life and relationships interesting.

It is my view that death merely adds another dimension to our relationships.

The end of the body does not destroy the living soul. Those that were, still are and don't have to be lost to you.

Those who have passed over are getting on with their new existence. So to really comprehend how our relationship with them from now on will work, we have to try to visualise their new life. We have talked a lot about how we are going to continue our lives. We also need to think about how they are going to continue with their lives.

Why do we need to do this, some people ask? Well, let me answer that by asking another question. Here in this earthly life, would you want to deny someone the right to live their life to the fullest? Would you want to stop them experiencing all the possibilities this world has available to them? I hope the answer is no, you wouldn't.

It is the same now that you are separated. Our grief and our inability to let go of that grief can impede and hold back our loved ones as they begin the great adventure that is life on the other side. They can be so concerned about us and the unhappiness that we are experiencing that they are bound in to us. They spend their time watching over us, making sure we are all right.

This is not something we should want for either of us. This is where our grief becomes selfish, where we become obsessive and possessive of it.

So we must all ask ourselves some questions here. Are we impeding their life on the other side? Are they having to constantly check up on us or watch over us because of the way we are failing to move on? Are we making them do the one thing that human relationships are not supposed to be about? Are we forcing them to be with us twenty-four hours a day?

Those are the dynamics of the relationship we are creating if we don't move on. So we must all look carefully inside ourselves and ask: 'Are my thoughts and my words and my actions not only stopping me from progressing but stopping them moving on as well? Am I being possessive?'

I remember one of the most selfish things that anyone ever said to me when I was giving them a reading was when a husband came through to his wife. He was being very communicative and was expressing the truth in a very caring and clear way. 'He wants you to know it's not goodbye but he has to get on with his existence too,' I said.

The lady looked at me and said simply: 'Well, I don't want him to. I don't want him to move away from me.'

I thought how tragic it was. That was the real tragedy of his passing. She was so possessive that she couldn't move on.

We must all ensure that we are not obsessive or possessive of the person who has passed over.

The best way for me to explain this to you is by giving you an example of how an obsessive attitude can inhibit the spirit of someone who has passed over. Fortunately, this particular example also illustrates how, by addressing this issue, we can all set our loved ones free to move on in their new existence.

In the first series of my television show *6ixth Sense* I passed on a message to a lady who had lost her son. It was a very emotional connection, perhaps one of the most memorable I have given.

The young man had died tragically young of a heart attack. As with all deaths that come out of absolutely nowhere, it had left his family—and his mother, in particular—absolutely devastated.

It was almost a year after her son's passing that the lady came to the studio to appear in my show. I could tell she was still very fragile. Despite this, however, when I connected to her son, he had—what seemed at the time—quite a harsh message to deliver to her.

It emerged that in the months since his death, the mother had been visiting the grave virtually every day. She was spending hours there, chatting away to him. Not only that, but she had surrounded the grave with flowers and candles. There were lighted candles there virtually all the time. The place had been converted into a shrine. It was, apparently, the same in the house, which was covered in photographs and memorabilia connected with her son. Before his death there had been the normal scattering of images of him around the house. Now there were dozens and dozens of photographs in every room. His old room was exactly as it was the day he died. Not a thing had been touched or moved.

The message I passed on to her was twofold. Of course, he was pleased to see her and happy to tell

her that he was safe and well on the other side. But he also wanted to let her know how her obsessive behaviour was affecting him in this new existence.

'Thanks for the candles, Mum, but there's no need for them every day,' he said. 'And there is no need for so many photos of me around the house either.'

She was slightly taken aback by this, but he explained why. 'It is stifling me,' he said. 'This communication can't continue if you stifle me. If you continue with this you will stifle me by being obsessed with my memory.'

The good news was that we did a follow-up with the lady a year later. She had moved on with her life in a very positive way. She still went to her son's grave, obviously. But the candles had gone, as had the photographs. And she only visited once a month or so.

It was the same in her house. His bedroom had been cleared of all his things. She had got rid of all his clothes and books. Instead of having photographs and reminders of her son everywhere, she'd put together a single collage of photographs which she kept in one corner of her living room.

But as well as this she'd moved on with her life. And she had done so in a way that kept her close to her son. She had, for instance, become closer to her son's fiancée. Their relationship had been difficult in the immediate aftermath of his passing. They had both been devastated by his loss and missed him in their own different ways.

Now they were developing a good relationship. She had also started seeing some of his friends. Again, it was a way of helping her to see that he was very much alive through the associations he had with other people. As she went through this process she told us that she had stopped being so bound in her grief. As a result, she said she felt closer to her son now than she had done since he passed over.

If you think about it, this makes perfect sense.

If we if hold on to the memory of a person, if we fix it in time in the way that this lady did, we are excluding everything that happened after their passing. And as a result we are stuck. We are stuck with that point of memory.

The comparison would be going round to see a friend or a member of the family on a daily basis and having the exact same conversation over and over and over again. The friendship probably would soon fade if you did that.

As I said earlier, relationships are dynamic, even when one half of that relationship has moved on to the other side. They need to move on, they need to grow. All relationships are built on new experiences. And if we no longer go on and have new experiences our relationships become stagnant, stuck in a point in time. And they will die.

Acts of Remembrance

Our ultimate goal is to keep those who have passed over close at all times. To do this we must prepare for both of us moving on with our existences.

This may take time.

To begin this process we need to move beyond the grieving period and begin to formalise the way in which we are going to remember our loved ones. Until now we have not confronted our need to do this, to mark their passing on a regular basis. We have been avoiding it. No longer. We need an act of remembrance.

Acts of remembrance
How are we going to go about remembering this person? How are we going to acknowledge their life? What tributes can we make that are fitting to their memory?

There are infinite options. We can do what most people do and make regular visits to their grave or final resting place. We can keep a pot of ashes on the sideboard. But we also choose to do neither of these things. We can do something more symbolic.

We could perhaps plant a tree. Or get a portrait of our loved one commissioned. We could choose a particular piece of music or a movie as a means of remembering the person who has passed over.

Alternatively, we could do something more appropriate for the way in which they passed over. If, for instance, our loved one died of cancer, we could decide to make a small, annual donation to a cancer charity around the time of their passing each year. *What* we do is much less important than the fact that we *do* something to remember them.

How often do you do this act of remembrance?
We are always going to be remembering them in our hearts and minds. But we do need to put aside a certain amount of time to fulfil our act of remembrance. There is a fine line to be walked between honouring someone's memory and obsessing about it. So we also have to decide how often we are going to remember them.

So how often should we enact it?

This is going to be a fluid thing, so you might want to go more frequently to begin with. Once a week, or perhaps the last Sunday of each month, depending on how you feel about the frequency of your visits. Whatever it is, you have to develop a routine around it, however. You mustn't avoid going. After that I would try to encourage people to make it an annual visit and perhaps birthdays.

It also has to be something that evolves into a celebratory and a warm event rather than a solemn event.

Initially you will need support to do this. But ultimately you need to move towards a time when you can do this alone or with the person who is most closely involved, perhaps a friend or another family member.

Don't over-elaborate your remembrance
As painful as it is, I would encourage people not to build shrines.

During the early days of the mourning process large displays of flowers and photographs can be a great solace. Memorials like this are becoming commonplace now. We often see friends and relatives, and even people who have little connection to the person who has passed, erecting elaborate memorials when someone dies in a road accident or a murder. These can be helpful in easing people through their initial sense of loss. But they can only serve a short-term purpose.

It is the same within the home. It is normal to fill the house with photographs and mementoes of someone who has passed over in the early days. But to keep them around long term is not helpful. A few treasured photos are fine, of course. But building and keeping permanent shrines to a loved one is a retrograde step.

Similarly, refusing to clear out their personal possessions and clothes isn't a good thing. Nor is it advisable to keep the person's bedroom as it was when they passed over. I know this is a painful thing, especially in the case of children who have passed over. Parents find it extremely hard to remove tangible evidence of the earthly life, the posters, the toys, the clothes. But they must do so. Keeping them only amplifies the sense of separation. It doesn't bring us closer, despite what people think. In fact it does the opposite. It stifles our loved ones as they begin their spirit existence and will, in the long term, inhibit our ability to connect with them.

Something to Celebrate

'Is my son happy, Colin?'

The heartfelt question came from a lady in the audience at a show in London. It caught me off guard a little as I'd been answering more general questions about mediumship and communicating with the spirit world.

I was happy to respond though. 'Well, the easiest way to answer that is by asking you a question,' I said. 'What was his personality like when he was here? Was he a happy boy?'

'Yes. Very happy,' his mother replied.

Based on this I explained to her that the chances were that he was happy in the spirit world too. I then went on to tell her why. 'The personality we have in this life is unaffected when we reach the other side,' I said. 'The basic character does not change but continues to evolve. So if your lad was a happy boy on this side of life he is the same way on the other side.'

This seemed to give the lady some reassurance.

As I was explaining this to her, however, I became aware of a presence, that of a young boy. I wasn't sure if he was connected to her or not. But I knew that he was showing me a moment at which his family had recently gathered around a montage of photographs of him.

'Would you understand that?' I asked.

The lady nodded. 'Yes, I would,' she said.

The boy then showed me a very specific date, 3 October. 'He is also showing me something you said at that time,' I explained. 'You said: "Now we are going to start celebrating his life."'

'That's right,' she agreed.

'He is telling me that you said: "Now we can move on."'

'That's right,' she said again.

'He is also telling me that, in terms of respect for his memory, that was the best thing you could have done,' I said.

The lady, who was crying, nodded her head in agreement. 'Thank you,' she said.

I could see that this had been a comfort to the lady but, given the suddenness of the connection, I didn't expect to be able to tell her much more.

The young boy didn't want to go away, however. 'He is telling me that he misses something you used to cook for him. It's either a lasagne or a shepherd's pie. He says it always used to be soggy,' I said.

She laughed. 'Shepherd's pie, yes,' she said, smiling.

'He misses your shepherd's pies,' I said. 'He misses the way you used to make them so that the gravy came up over the side of the dish.'

The lady was getting very emotional now, as indeed was her son—and so was I too. I could tell that he had gone to an enormous effort to get to me and that he desperately wanted to get one final message through to his mother.

'He wants to say four words to you,' I continued. 'They relate to something you said when he passed over. He wants to say, "I love you, Mum."'

The lady began crying uncontrollably at this, as did other members of the audience. 'That's what I said when he passed,' she explained. 'I said I would never hear him say, "I love you, Mum" again.'

'Well, you have heard it again,' I said. 'And he still does love you very much.'

It was a highly charged connection and one that left me and the audience deeply moved. Afterwards, however, I could see that she was extremely happy about the message, as were her friends who were all smiling and hugging her. It was as if they were saying: 'See, we told you so.'

I didn't get a chance to speak to her afterwards but it was clear to me that she was an example of a person who had benefited from moving on with her life. This lady had clearly been devastated by the loss of her boy. The grieving process had gone on for a long time. But, in the weeks before my show she had finally reached the point where she felt she could move on and celebrate his life.

As she did so the distance between her and her son closed. And she was able to receive a message from him that night. It illustrates something that I have said many times. To move on you need to draw a positive from the negative that is your loss.

This is, I know, a very difficult thing to do. People say to me: 'That's easy for you to say.' And they are right, it is. But it is easy because I know it is true. I have seen it proved time and time again.

The loss of a child is perhaps the most difficult of all things to cope with. Many parents I meet find it incredibly difficult to deal with.

Over the years, I have spoken to the mothers and fathers of many children who have passed over. Often they have left this life in terrible circumstances, some in the worst way of all, having been murdered.

What I try to tell each of these parents is that they should strive to reach a point where they can celebrate the life they had with that child. I try to encourage them to take a positive, to see some good in what has happened. This is, of course, tough. More often than not they say to me: 'But there is no good in this. How on earth can I take a positive from something that is so negative?'

My reply is always the same: 'I know you can't see it now, but there is good in it and that good lies in the fact that for however many years it was, you played your part in making that child the person they were. You did your bit to raise and educate someone of whom so many people are now saying, "What a good person they were. Isn't it tragic that something like this has happened to a person like that?" That is something that is definitely worth celebrating.'

PART FOUR

A New Beginning

If we have confronted and dealt with death in our earthly lives, then what comes after death should be a great, exciting and life-affirming new experience too.

The Parting of the Ways

The more I learn about the afterlife, the more I grow to love that wonderful line from *Peter Pan*, the original play by J. M. Barrie: 'To die will be an awfully big adventure.' The more I communicate with those who have passed over to the spirit world, the more I begin to see that death really must be an 'awfully big adventure'. And not only for those in the afterlife.

I believe that the line actually applies to both sides of life. If we have confronted and dealt with death in our earthly lives, then what comes after death should be a great, exciting and life-affirming new experience too.

This is how we should move on with our lives from now on. We should view this moment as a—temporary—parting of the ways. We must learn to let those who have passed over set off on their awfully big adventure. And we must ensure that our new life is an awfully big adventure too.

Don't Be Possessive

Lots of people talk about setting our loved ones free when they have passed over. To be honest, that's a bit poetic and airy-fairy for me. It's a bit wishy-washy. I think it's more realistic and practical than that. To me it's about acknowledging the fact that we don't possess them.

We have talked about how some people can be obsessive of the memory of the person who has passed over. They can also be possessive of the person.

So at this point we have to take a look at ourselves again. We need to acknowledge that we never owned the person in life and we certainly don't own them in death. And therefore you cannot bind them to you or feel them closer to you by thinking of them as someone you own or possess.

You have to face up to the fact that, even if it was a child that you brought into this world, you never owned that person. The time they spent with you was time they chose to share with you.

A person in a deep state of grief often isn't very good at acknowledging that other people could be grieving as well. They don't seem to understand that the grief a friend feels at someone's passing can be just as intense as that of the dead person's wife, husband, parents or children.

Others show their possessiveness by openly resenting the fact that other people are talking about their loved ones. They say: 'How dare you talk about them—they were my friend, my partner, my husband.'

Alternatively, they claim some sort of bragging rights. They imply that their grief is somehow more important. People who do this say things like: 'Oh yes, but you didn't know them as well as I did.' It's as if to say: 'You may be missing them but you can't possibly be missing them as much as I am.'

That is being possessive. It is not productive for you and it is not productive for the person who has passed over either.

A Distant Shore

We have to acknowledge that just as in earthly life, those people who have passed on have an existence that they have to experience and to live. It's almost like someone emigrating to another country. It's a good way of thinking about those who have passed over. They have decided to take a path away from you. You can still speak to them on the phone or email them, but the physical side of them isn't available. It's as if a certain percentage of their being isn't there any more. It might be ten per cent of them, it might be twenty-five per cent. It doesn't really matter how much it is. The key thing is that a part of them is not there.

When you are going to rejoin them is, of course, going to depend on your mortality. But for the period until you can rejoin them eighty or ninety per cent of them has moved away to a distant shore. It is the ten or twenty per cent that remains with you that you need to concentrate on.

*   *   *

The most common question I'm asked is: 'What does the afterlife look like?'

I am always wary of answering this question. This is partly because, even if I had been given a clear vision of what it is like, to do so would give people a fixed definition of something that is highly personal. This would, I believe, inhibit their ability to grow personally and spiritually. So my reply is always the same. I'm not capable of seeing eternity and nor is anybody. I can only tell you what I've seen. And what I've seen is an environment which reflects what people want their afterlife to look like.

Let me give you an example. I have an uncle with whom I have connected several times since he passed over. When I have an experience with him he always appears to me sitting in a window in his favourite armchair. I may be wrong here, but I suspect this must be something he has created through his own consciousness.

Not everything I have seen there is as tangible and recognisable from this earthly life, of course. At other times I have been shown colours that don't exist in this world. I have found myself listening to music that is beyond anything you can hear in this existence. On other occasions, the experience I have is almost hallucinogenic. What the spirits I am in contact with when I see and hear these things are doing is projecting on to me their experience of the afterlife. Given all this, I have come to think of the afterlife as being a multidimensional state.

And within that multi-faceted state, the law of attraction seems to work. People are drawn to things according to how they have evolved so they are drawn towards things that they comprehend and reflect how they think.

People ask me, 'Is there a hell?' I think people may get the afterlife they deserve but I also think people are capable of transforming on the other side, of changing into something more than they were on this earthly plane. You can see that it has happened on this side of life. Take someone like John McVicar, a hardened criminal who has transformed himself into this very calm, philosophical champion of human rights. But I digress.

The afterlife is very much a personal experience. For those who have passed over, it's an existence of their own creation.

People sometimes say to me, 'That sounds a bit like Never Never Land.'

My answer is: 'Well, look around you.' This is a world of our own creation too. Someone built the house that you are living in. Someone put up the fence in your garden. Someone planted the tree in your park. Someone laid your road, built your chair, knitted your jumper. We live in a physical world, so the process of building things is slower here. If you want a house on the other side you simply think it. It's not so different. Just faster.

One of the things I've realised about mediumship over the years is that everything is at a much faster pace in the spirit dimension. And that means that the medium's mind tends to go into a much faster phase when we are working. Many people have that experience where they see something flash past them. Or a thought hurtles through their mind so fast they are left saying, 'What was that?' This is the closest people get to the mediumistic experience.

Because it is free of the density of matter, the spirit world operates much quicker. If there is a substance—call it ether or whatever—then it responds to the power of consciousness. It doesn't actually require physical labour to construct things. It requires mental labour.

The reason we all need to understand these things is this. Just as in this earthly life, people must be given room to evolve, to develop. They must have the space to build their world around them. This, again, is why it is vitally important that we are not possessive of the person that has passed over. We must allow them their space.

Create New Associations

If our new life is to be an awfully great adventure, then it needs to be a challenge. So the first thing we must do as we enter this phase is to set ourselves a very specific challenge. We must do something or go somewhere that we associate with the person who has passed over. Our goal is to create a new association, to put a new slant on something familiar.

We are, once again, trying to turn a weakness into a strength. We want to replace the current negative and backward-looking association with a newer, more positive and forward-looking one. We need it to be an association that doesn't involve us being with the person who has passed over.

How do we do this?

For some people this might be difficult so it is best to make it a firm commitment rather than a vague promise. Commit yourself to doing something on a specific day at a specific time. Then decide on what it is you're going to do to create your positive experience.

There are, of course, endless possibilities here.

For example, you could go to a restaurant that you used to visit with your husband or wife or partner. Perhaps when you went there you always used to have the same meal or sit at the same table. Go back to the same restaurant but this time do something different. Sit at a different table.

Have something you've not had before. Take someone along who has never been there before. Whatever you do make it different and make it an enjoyable experience.

Alternatively, if you used to go for a particular walk with the person who has passed over, go out on that walk again. But this time, take a detour, shorten or extend the walk, or, if it's a circuitous route, walk in the opposite direction to the one you used to walk. If you don't feel up to doing it on your own, take someone with you. This in itself will create new associations that will help you.

It really doesn't matter what you do. The important thing is that you do something. The key is that you are recreating a familiar experience but changing it somehow. In doing so you are recognising, in a small way, that you are moving on.

The benefits will be great. You will come away having faced the experience and realising that you could face it again and again and again. And you should do it again. Each time you do so, do it with a different friend or a different family member. Each occasion you go back you will have taken a significant and positive step forward.

*　　　　*　　　　*

I know this is a step that some people find difficult. Memories are powerful, and you can't erase the old associations simply overnight. Nor would you want to. But it is an exercise that, I know from experience, helps people enormously as they move on with their lives.

Let me recount two brief encounters that, I

hope, demonstrate what I mean.

At a show in the north of England one evening I got a message from a man who was trying to get in touch with his wife. It was a very warm message, nothing dramatic particularly. He just wanted to tell his wife that he loved her and that she was doing well in moving on with her life.

The thing that stuck in my mind, and produced a ripple of laughter around the audience, was when he was talking to his wife about her going to their favourite restaurant—an Indian restaurant called the Star of India, I think.

They used to go there once a month, without fail. And once a month, without fail, they would have the same dishes. Communicating through me in the theatre that evening, the husband starting laughing about the fact that she had been back to the Star of India.

'He's laughing because you had what you want, not what he thought you wanted,' I told her.

She was sitting in the audience with her sister. They both burst out laughing, as did the rest of the audience.

'Do you understand that?'

'Yes I do,' she said.

It turned out that every time they went to the restaurant her husband would always order a particular dish for his wife. She always used to say how lovely it was. But actually, she confessed, she didn't like it very much. Each month she had it because it was what he thought she liked. She didn't say anything because she didn't want to upset his feelings.

A similar thing happened at another show, this time in the West Country, where again a husband came through wanting to communicate with his wife.

He began showing me images of the holidays they used to have in Spain each year. They were clearly very happy memories and, as he described them, his wife was smiling.

He too was a man with a lovely sense of humour, which came through towards the end of the reading. 'He has one last thing to say to you before he goes,' I told the lady. 'He says you can "bloody well go to Greece now". Do you know what that means?' I said.

'Oh yes, we went to Spain every year because he liked it,' she said. 'I liked it too but I always fancied going to Greece one year, just for a change, but he wouldn't have it.'

As it turned out she had already booked her holiday for that summer. To Greece.

As in the case of the husband who had laughed at his wife going to the curry house, this man's message was one of approval. He was pleased that his wife was doing what she wanted to do. She was living with his memory but also living in the present.

Rearrange the Furniture

Years ago, early in my career, I occasionally used to go to people's houses and do private sittings. I remember vividly a visit I made to the home of Margaret, a lady who lived in a town near the south coast of England. She was a relatively young-looking woman, perhaps in her mid-fifties.

Margaret invited me into her living room and asked me to sit down. Without really thinking about it I plonked myself in a rather comfortable-looking leather chair in the corner of the room. The moment I did this, the woman's face took on a slightly shocked look. 'Oh, that's John's chair,' she said. 'You're the first person who has sat in John's chair since he passed away.'

'I'm sure he won't mind me sitting here,' I smiled. 'And to be quite honest he doesn't need it any more.'

She laughed, a little nervously. 'No, I suppose he doesn't.'

When I began the sitting her husband, John, came through and connected with me. It was a very good reading. It was clear they had been a very devoted couple who did everything together. A lot of the communication between them related to their life together in this home. He asked about the garden and the new kitchen he'd apparently fitted a few years ago.

They were all little things that pleased her, but then I saw John showing me something that made her pause for thought.

'He is telling me that you should change the covers on the three-piece suite,' I told Margaret. 'He says it's time you brightened it up a bit.'

'Oh, OK,' she said, shifting nervously in the chair. 'I didn't think he wanted me to change anything, but if that's what he wants then I will.'

Sometimes the most profound messages are contained in the smallest, seemingly most insignificant details. So it was here.

Speaking to Margaret over a cup of tea after I'd finished the reading, she told me that she had steadfastly refused to change anything in the house after John had died. 'I have left everything exactly the way he liked it,' she said, rather proudly. Sure enough when I looked around I could see that John's Wellington boots were still standing by the back door, John's jacket was still hanging on a peg on the back of the door.

The mistake she'd made was one that many people make. Quite wrongly, she'd assumed that by keeping things as they were, she would somehow keep some part of John in the house.

I explained to her that, in fact, her actions were achieving the exact opposite effect. We had managed to connect him to her today, but I told her I doubted they would communicate often if she didn't have more to say to him. How many conversations could they have about the colour of the kitchen cabinets or whether the leaky tap had been fixed?

For him to connect with her in a meaningful way, he needed her to move on. She needed to make the house reflect the future, not the past. She needed to change the furniture, in every sense. As gently as he could, that's what he had been saying in his message. He had mentioned the three-piece suite but, in fact, he meant the whole house needed to come to life again.

I told Margaret that she was trapped in time. Everything had stopped when John had died.

'You really need to move on from that,' I said.

She assured me that she would. She even said she was going to sit in John's chair herself from now on.

Envision the Future

As we take our first, tentative steps out into the world, we can't predict what the future is going to be. We can't say in a year's time we will be doing this and this is exactly how we are going to do it. Nobody is expecting any of us to be a seer or a prophet at this point. But we can begin to think in general terms about what may happen in the future.

A good way to think of it is to compare it to planning our pensions. I know that sounds rather boring but bear with me.

We are all encouraged to make provisions for the future with our pensions. What none of us can tell is how many of us are going to get to pensionable age. What do we say to that? Do we not bother? Do we say we might not reach pensionable age, so there's no point in planning for that eventuality? But then what happens if we do? What are we going to do then? It is too late to start planning then.

The same thing applies here, in a sense. We have to have some vision of what our future is going to be. We can't say when it is going to happen. We can't say who is going to be involved in it. But we can begin to get a picture of what it might look like.

It is important, however, that we are realistic. So, whilst we might, at this point, begin to think to ourselves that we could envisage eventually finding a new life partner, for instance, we can't be too specific.

The fact of the matter is that no one is going to

be able to fill the place of the partner you have lost because that relationship was unique. But what we can start saying is that we are going to start liv ing a life where we will meet new people, perhaps form new friendships, even new meaningful relationships.

You may have lost a child. In that case you may say I am going to have another child at some point in the future. As long as you realise that child is never going to replace the one that has passed over. It is going to be another child.

I do find it sad when people lose a child and they give it the same name as the one they have lost. They say it is a tribute. But the inescapable truth of the matter is you can't replace the child that was lost.

This is typical of a common mistake that people make at this point—trying to replicate that which they have lost. I come across many men and women who have lost their life partners and say: 'I am going to find a man who is exactly like my husband or find a woman who is exactly like my wife.' This is when things do go horribly wrong. We are planting the seeds of disaster when we rush out and find someone who is exactly like our previous partner or—even worse—someone we think we can make or mould into an exact replica of that partner. If we go down that path then we can be certain of one thing: we will be crying our eyes out in a few years' time.

And it won't be the fault of the person with whom we have rushed into a relationship. The truth is we can't find easy replacements for those we have loved and lost. Nor should we want to. Think how hard it was to find that person you have lost in the first place.

We have to understand that we are going into new relationships, with new rules, new boundaries, new experiences. So as we prepare to head off on this new adventure where we are going out and embracing life again, we have to accept that these new relationships are going to be different.

The Madonna Syndrome

We are all embarking on a new and exciting life.

It will embrace and acknowledge the past but it will involve us primarily looking to the future and the new existence we are going to shape for ourselves.

We must, however, go slowly here. It is not a time to reinvent ourselves like Madonna. Yes, we must go out and be brave enough to experience the unfamiliar and the new. But we must not go wild. We must not charge into things.

A lot of people make rash decisions when they emerge from bereavement. Often when people lose a partner they give all their money away to their children. They say: 'Oh, I won't need that any more because my life is ended.' This is not wise.

As I say, this is potentially an exciting time in our lives. As the veil of sadness lifts, we can begin to look forward to a new and rewarding life. But as we look forward to the future we can still be guided by the past.

So at this early stage in our new life, it is often helpful to let our loved ones guide us a little. We want their influence to live on, after all, so we can draw on their help by asking questions like:

- What would they have wanted me to do now?
- What would they have wanted us to do together?
- How would they have lived if it had been me that had passed over?
- What were their long-term dreams and do they still fit in with mine?

You are not going to achieve this overnight. And a lot of it is going to have to be trial and error.

Trying to establish this path, setting yourself goals, moving beyond grief and feeling that sense of connection, is really about putting yourself in situations and circumstances and seeing if they work for you. But it is also about putting yourself in the right places at this point.

It's rather like an example I use in positive thinking: if you are a very quiet, studious, bookish kind of person looking to meet a perfect partner, you are not going to find them in a nightclub.

An acquaintance of mine has gone through a succession of relationships although she is only in her late thirties. She has married three times and had several long-term partners but they have all ended in absolute disaster. And she always ends up with the same type of waste-of-space man. She will split up with one and go straight back into the type of place and situation where she had met the previous man, usually in a nightclub when she's had too much to drink. Then she can never work out why men keeping treating her like dirt. The reason is that she keeps putting herself in circumstances where she is going to meet only men

124

who will treat her like dirt.

Finding this path is a bit like that. You have to look in the right places.

So at this point it is wise not to try anything too adventurous. But at the same time you can begin to impose your own personality on what you do. If, for instance, you and your partner used to do a favourite country walk, why not head out on that walk but take a slightly different route. This way you are literally looking for a new path. Alternatively you might want to join a ramblers' group.

Whatever it is you choose to do, patience is important. It is important also not to be too hard on yourself. If you do something and it turns out to be an experience that brings back an uncomfortable memory or brings a moment of sadness, don't be put off. Don't let one or two bad experiences lead you into saying: 'I'm never trying that again, this is never going to work out.' You run the risk of making yourself feel inadequate and heightening your sense of aloneness.

The important thing about trying new paths is that you will eventually stumble upon one that leads you to a place where you can begin to grow as a person and find a new sense of perspective on life. And you simply must understand that this won't come immediately. It's about experimentation. Seeing if you can cope with the situation. It's not about impersonating Madonna.

Nothing is Lost

Some people do emerge from their bereavement determined to transform their life in a day. To me, that is like trying to eat the whole cake all in one go. Anyone who tries to take this all on in one go is going to make themselves physically and spiritually sick.

Every now and again you see something on television that leaves you speechless. I saw one such programme quite recently. It was about young widows and how they were coming to terms with losing their husbands.

It isn't often that I feel like climbing into the television, grabbing hold of someone on the screen and leading them to safety. I did on this occasion though.

One of the women had been absolutely devoted to her husband who had died very tragically of cancer. Theirs had clearly been a very genuine and committed marriage. Yet within a few months of his death she was getting ready to marry a man she had met off the internet.

As she prepared for the wedding, the cameras followed her around. In my opinion, the number of mistakes she was making was quite staggering. It seemed clear that she hadn't acknowledged her husband, to whom she had obviously been absolutely devoted. Every now and again you would catch a glimpse of her staring off into space at the mention of his name. It seemed obvious she still had strong feelings for him.

Then, literally hiding at the back of the sofa, the cameras watched as she packed away all the mementoes she had of their wedding and their marriage into a large box. It was going to be put into an attic in the new home she was moving to with her new husband.

She had sold the old home in the space of a week. It was as if she was denying her previous life

126

had ever existed. You didn't need to be a psychic to be able to predict where this was going. It was going to end in tears. To me, it was a classic example of something that many of us are guilty of—denying that which has made us what we are.

*   *   *

Moving on is not about filling your life up with new things. It *is* about resolving issues and finding new paths. And it is also about valuing and putting into proper perspective what you used to have in your life.

I made this mistake myself a few years ago, when I split up with my partner of many years, Chris. I had realised I couldn't stay in the relationship any more. It wasn't good for me and it wasn't good for him. So he moved out, leaving me in the home we had shared together.

The moment I had the house to myself I began erasing every trace of its previous life. I had a new carpet laid. I had laminate flooring put in all the way through the kitchen and dining room. I redecorated. I bought a new bed and sofa.

But then I remember one particular night, sitting there thinking, 'I am on my own.' And I was really frightened. I realised that I had been in a relationship since I was sixteen. I had a panic. I didn't know what to do.

I would have been forty years old at the time, but for six months I went out and tried to live my life as if I was still twenty. Then, one night, when I was feeling a little more philosophical about the way I'd been behaving and the changes I'd made, I decided to compare what I was doing with the actions I was counselling bereaved people to take. There are strong similarities between bereavement and the end of a serious relationship. I thought: 'Come on, apply your philosophy to your own life.'

I realised that I had been trying to catch up on all those 'lost' years. But it turned out they weren't lost years after all. Even though not all of those twenty-five years was perfect, I wouldn't have been the person I was now had I not experienced that twenty-five-year relationship. Suddenly I realised I couldn't throw those years away. I had learned something from them, I had taken a great deal of value from them. Even though there were lots of reasons we had split up I had to be grateful to Chris because he was a huge part of making me the person I am.

It was at that point that I began to salvage a friendship with him. I had by now thrown away much of the material stuff that we had accumulated together. But I thought I can't throw this person away.

From that moment on, I knew that he would remain an important person in my life. It was just that he was not going to be an important person in the same way. As I say, divorce and separation are for many people akin to a major bereavement.

As we move on we must be careful not to throw the person we loved away.

Perception: How to Avoid Being a Merry Widow

A while back, I was having dinner with a good friend of mine, Hannah. It was one of those memorable evenings where the wine and the conversation flowed. Just as it should between friends.

It was lovely to see her enjoying herself so much. Her husband, David, to whom she had been devoted, had died around eighteen months earlier. It had taken her some time to deal with the pain of bereavement and to pick up with me and other close members of her social circle again.

We were talking about the new social life she was enjoying when she said something that I thought was very telling. 'I've been out quite a few times now,' she confided. 'But the trouble with going out with my friends since David passed over is that they treat me like a grieving widow.'

'That's probably a perception thing,' I replied.

'What do you mean?' she wondered, looking quizzical.

'I mean you're being treated like a grieving widow because you are presenting yourself as one. If you want to be treated as just another one of the girls, then you have to present yourself as just one of the girls.'

'I will,' she said, with a knowing wink. 'And I think I know just the dress to do it in!'

Hannah's experience is something that I encounter very often. As they re-emerge into the world after bereavement, many people tell me that they feel pigeonholed, stereotyped as widows or widowers. When they take their first steps back into their old social circle everyone behaves as if they are walking on eggshells, terrified of offending or upsetting them. Whenever this happens I tell them the same thing as I told Hannah: perception is everything.

The TV comedy show *Little Britain* hit this particular nail on the head when they did a sketch about a girl who was, coincidentally enough, getting over the death of her boyfriend David. She represented an extreme that even I haven't seen, thankfully!

Everything anyone ever said or did reminded her of her David. When her sister came round and asked if she wanted a coffee she burst into tears. 'That's what David used to say to me,' she balled. Whenever the sister did something else equally mundane, she'd get the same reaction. 'That's what David used to do,' the grieving character would weep. Understandably the sister got more and more frustrated with her.

I have encountered people who have wallowed in their misery a little like this. There is no getting away from it. It's a harsh thing and you can say it with a compassionate smile on your face, but eventually someone has to say, actually people are getting fed up with you banging on.

People will only treat you according to how you behave. So it is important that you set the rules for those who are around you.

The key thing you need to do here is to decide in advance how you want people to perceive you and then act accordingly. First impressions are last impressions, so you can do a lot simply by giving out the right visual signals. For instance, I would avoid dressing head to toe in black. Even if it was your normal fashion before your bereavement. It's also important that you at least try to look relaxed. Even if you feel tense. If you look uptight then that is going to be picked up by everyone else. And that will soon lead to the sort of walking-on-eggshells conversations that you want to avoid. It's a question of trying to achieve that balance again.

Verbally too you can set the mood yourself from

the beginning. When you rejoin your social circle you can immediately start setting the boundaries of how you want other people to treat your grief simply by saying: 'Look, it's OK if you talk about the person who has passed over but it doesn't have to be the topic of conversation for the entire evening. I am out to have a fun time, after all.'

Your friends are your friends for a reason, remember. Trust them to respond as friends.

Say What You Mean

As well as working as a medium, I spend a lot of time coaching people in positive thinking. It's something I believe in passionately. There are many aspects of positive thinking that apply to the process we are going through here, but one of the most important is the language we use. The words we use are incredibly important.

When I am teaching positive thinking, for instance, there is a word that I always ban in my lectures. The word is 'but'. There are no 'buts' in my lectures. 'Buts are for sitting on,' I say. 'If I make a statement to you I hope you will embrace it and use it to change your life. There are no buts.'

The same thing applies now as you immerse yourself back in the world. The words you use go a long way towards deciding how you are perceived. Let me give you a few examples of what I mean here:

Don't say 'lost'
It's quite common for people to talk of having lost a loved one. I hate that word and recommend people avoid it all cost. Why? What's wrong with it? Well,

it's simple. You haven't lost them. They've simply moved on. You can't see them at present, however that doesn't mean you won't be able to find them at some point in the future. That's what this book is all about—finding them. So, using the word lost implies you can't conceive of any way that you can actually find them. Don't let that perception take root. Don't say lost. If you continue that attitude you will never find that path that may lead to you finding them.

Don't say 'passed away'
That implies they've gone somewhere from where they won't return. It also implies somewhere that you don't know. By saying they have passed over, however, you are making it clear that you know they have gone somewhere specific. It implies that you know what they have passed over to. This creates a far more positive perception.

Avoid using negative phrases
Don't say things like: 'I will never get over him.' Or: 'No one will ever fill her place.' By the very nature of how you've said it, you've decided that no one ever will. You will define the perceptions of everyone around you. It will make them believe you are incapable of moving on—with them or anyone else.

PART FIVE

Purpose

There is no point in carrying on for the sake of carrying on. You have to carry on with meaning, with purpose.

No More Tears

It is time to take stock. It's time to ask ourselves some simple questions, such as, what is our long-term goal? What is the life that we ultimately want to lead as we move on? And how do we want to share that life with those who have passed over?

Everyone's goals are going to be different. They will reflect their circumstances as well as their ability and willingness to make changes in their life. But in general I believe we each need to aspire to achieve four things.

1. To eliminate the grief and the sense of separation that weighs us down when we face the passing of someone close.
2. To replace those feelings with a sense of a complete but separate life.
3. To feel that we are still living our life to the full with memories and separate experiences but also some experiences that we share with those who have passed over to the spirit side.
4. To be able to deal with those latter experiences positively, to be able to face them with a smile on our face rather than a tear in our eye.

I believe this is something that everyone can achieve, but, of course, it's not always that easy.

No More Small Picture

There are some passings that, no matter how hard we try, are never going to make sense. *Why did my child die of a one-in-a-million illness? Why was my husband killed on the way home from work?* We can, as we have seen, get utterly wrapped up, even trapped, in the circumstances of death. We can spend a lot of time trying to make sense of it, trying to understand the unfairness of it. We can, if we really wish, drive ourselves insane trying to do so.

But at this point we have to accept a hard truth. There are deaths that don't make sense and never will. At least in terms of the small picture. When you analyse it, most deaths don't make sense from this perspective. The proportion of people who have a 'good death' and pass away in bed, having fallen asleep at a very old age surrounded by everyone they love, is pretty small.

Most deaths involve unfair illness, accidents, acts of violence or natural tragedies. We only have to switch on the television news or pick up a newspaper to see them all around us. The child that is found face down in two inches of water. The parents who have murdered their children because divorce has left them separated. The desperate fathers who have said: 'If I can't have them neither can you.' One recent case that struck me as particularly upsetting: the woman who murdered her child because she couldn't bear the stigma of the infant's disability. How is she going to live with that on her conscience? That is a subject for another time and place.

To the families and friends connected and affected by each of those deaths, they make absolutely no sense whatsoever. Those people could spend the rest of their lives trying to make sense of it but they won't succeed.

So at this point we have to make a permanent change. We have to commit to a fundamental shift in our attitude to what has happened. Whatever the circumstances of someone's passing, no matter what age they were and no matter how tragic the events surrounding their passing, we have to get past that point where we keep asking ourselves 'why?' If we continue to get caught up in the question of 'why' we will never move on.

What we have to understand now is that there is no sense, justice, fairness, call it what you will, if you continue to see the small picture. The only way forward is to look beyond that and look at the bigger picture. The small picture is a bleak picture. But the bigger picture is much brighter. It's like the difference between squinting and trying to make sense of a black and white negative and seeing the same image printed and blown up into a panoramic view.

To get that image into our minds we must all think to ourselves: 'Their existence is carrying on so my existence has got to carry on too. The greatest tribute that I can pay to that person is to carry on.'

Again, we must also picture what is going on in their new existence, how they are progressing in their new world. So we must say: 'They've got to embrace life in the other dimension, so I have to embrace it in this dimension. I have to carry on. And I have to carry on with purpose.'

136

* * *

One of the faults I find with much bereavement advice is the way people are simply told they must 'carry on'. That is much, much too simple a statement. We have got to get on with life, it's true. But it's about the quality of that life. If we are to spend the rest of our earthly days plodding on, thinking solely that we have got to get through the mundane days we have left until our own mortality comes to an end, then the remainder of our existence is going to be thoroughly miserable. Quite frankly we are going to be more dead than those who have passed over.

There is no point in carrying on for the sake of carrying on. We have to carry on with meaning, with purpose.

At this point, it is important we ask ourselves some key questions again. They concern how we are now dealing with the circumstances that surrounded our loved one's passing over.

- Are your thoughts still focused on the circumstances of their passing?
- Are you still consoling yourself by constantly referring back to happier times?
- Do you still get upset and tearful when other people talk about the person who has passed over?
- Do you still discourage people from talking about them?
- Do people still feel uncomfortable talking about them in your presence?
- Are you still surrounded with more

mementoes of that person than you would have had if they were still physically here?
- Do you still avoid interacting with people?
- Are you still avoiding planning events in your life?

As we move into this next phase, we should give ourselves one single, simple purpose. To ensure that we will never answer yes to any of these questions again.

A New Purpose

Until we experience the shock of a major bereavement most of us have a fairly good idea of what we think life is going to be like in the future. We have a vision of the life we want for ourselves and our loved ones further down the road. Pursuing that vision gives our life meaning and purpose.

As couples, for instance, we talk about what we will do when the kids grow up, or when one or both of us retire. Our children talk about their hopes and dreams for what they will do when they leave school and go on to university or get their first job. Most of us have an overall vision of the things we hope to do with our lives. I certainly do. It mostly involves lying on a beach in Brazil!

However, when death takes an important person away from us, whether it's a child or partner or parent, it is very easy to lose that sense of direction. It is very easy to abandon that hope and that vision of where life is going. It is easy to lose your sense of purpose.

It is important, however, that we don't do that. We mustn't let death stop us wanting life. We mustn't lose that sense of purpose that we had. For their sake as much as ours.

As we re-emerged into the world, it was important that we kept things loose and unstructured. At that point we needed loose aims and targets, general aspirations for the future but no firm plans. All that must now change.

We must now make firm commitments and plans. And we must stick to them.

So, for instance, we may have decided which personal effects we are going to keep and which we are going to get rid of. To make sure we go through with this we must make a date to have a delivery van, a charity or a skip come to collect the unwanted stuff. If we are going to sell everything, we must book ourselves a date at a car boot sale. It doesn't really matter how we dispose of these things, what's important is that we do it.

Similarly, we must now start putting firm dates in the social diary. Book that holiday. Arrange that theatre trip with the grandchildren. Arrange events and decide who you are going to attend them with. Is it going to be a solo event or something shared? Start committing yourself. And as you do so start filling in the calendar on the kitchen wall with pen rather than pencil markings.

This is the point at which we can commit to those things that we want to do as part of our acknowledgement of our loved ones. So if we feel brave enough, now is the time to book that Caribbean cruise that you always talked about with your husband, wife or partner. Now is the time that you let other children play with your child's remaining toys when they come round to your house.

What we are doing here is making plans that keep the person's memory sacred to us, but no longer exclude other people from sharing our life. One of the best ways we can honour a person's memory is to engage with life in the way that the person would have wanted us to have done.

*   *   *

When a gentleman called Ken came through one evening he showed me that he wanted to get in contact with his granddaughter. She was sitting in the audience and her name was Tessa. It turned out that Tessa regarded Ken as her dad as well as her grandad. I sensed that there had been a fair bit of turmoil in the family and her real parents hadn't been around for her. Ken had effectively raised her.

I could tell from the images and thoughts he was giving me that Ken had been a great character. He seemed to be someone from the old school. Someone who lived by the old philosophy of living simply and within your means. I also got a sense that he was one of these people who didn't believe in leaving anything behind. 'Whatever is left after I'm gone you can burn it at the bottom of the garden,' he used to joke.

But inevitably, it is hard to leave this physical life without some unfinished business. You can rid yourself of the physical things that surround you, but clearing out the emotional clutter can be a lot harder. And so it had proved with Ken and his family.

Ken had suffered a lot towards the end. He was in terrible pain when he passed over. His final days had been hard, both for him and his family as he dealt with both his illness and the family's unfinished business. But when he came through he wanted to tell his granddaughter a couple of things that had been concerning him. 'I had to tell you about those things involving those papers and documents,' he said. This immediately struck a chord. I suggested it might be to do with her grandfather's estate but the lady told me it was in fact his daughter. 'It was to do with my mother,' she said.

Tessa confirmed that he had told her something important that she did not know about her mother. I didn't delve any further. I sensed that it related to the identity of her father.

The other thing he did was thank her for making sure too many people weren't around him at the end. 'You did a good job even though you think you didn't,' he said.

The connection was a great relief for Tessa. Like so many people, she had felt guilty about the way she had dealt with her loved one's final days. She wasn't sure that she had done the right thing in keeping Ken away from his many friends and relatives.

The thing that had pleased Ken the most, however, was the way that she had continued her life after his passing. In particular, she had used his passing to re-organise her life financially. I got the strong feeling that he had been a man who had preached the virtues of thrift and saving money. He didn't approve at all of the modern attitude to money, the 'spend it today, pay for it tomorrow' philosophy of the younger generation.

She smiled and nodded her head. It turned out that Tessa was once very much a member of the modern generation when it came to money matters. If she had wanted something in life she had gone out and got it, regardless of whether she had money in the bank. She had lived on credit cards. She had had huge debts on her credits cards, she admitted, but was clear of them all now.

'He's very pleased that you are much better with money now than you were when he was around,' I said.

As we have seen, when someone passes it can be a huge opportunity for us to tidy up our lives, to correct the things that deep down we know are wrong. But it also gives us all a chance to alter our lives—and those of others—for the better. The actions we take can be relatively small, personal changes, as in Tessa's case. Or they can be much grander gestures, life-changing measures that affect not just our own lives but the lives of others as well. The important thing is that we act with a meaning and a purpose that honours the memory of those who have passed over.

Spiritual Supporters

I often coach people in getting through this difficult transition into a fulfilling new life. One of the most important messages I have for them is this: you will have to face this new life on your own physically. But you don't have to face it on your own spiritually.

I am a great believer in the value and power of talking to those who are living on the other side. I do so during my readings, so why shouldn't everyone do it? There is nothing ever preventing you from talking to them whether you do that out loud or in your head. You can do that at any time.

What I encourage you to do is be perceptive enough that you can sense the reply. For example, the first time you are invited to a dinner party there is nothing wrong with you sitting down before you go out and talking to the person who has passed over and saying: 'Look, I'm going to this party. You know what's going to happen. It's the first time I've done this without you. I need to feel the confidence to let me do that. I know you were the one who always led the conversation when we went out. I'm going to need you to be around so that I'm strong enough to take the lead now.'

By expressing to them the things that you want to feel strong about, you will be able to gain the courage to just go out and do it knowing that something of them will be there with you.

I often coach people to do this, but you don't need a medium to help you. The simple task of talking to them can give you all the confidence you need. By doing so you can feel them.

The same is going to apply in other difficult circumstances. Take, for example, an instance where you are going to a children's party and seeing other children after the passing of your own child. You need to get the courage to go there without your child's physical presence. You need to tell yourself that the spirit of your child is there because you are there. Again you can face it physically on your own because you know that spiritually you are not alone.

As you move on, there is no circumstance that you can't apply that to. If you accept that something of them is still part of your life, then you can face anything physically on your own.

Someone Watching Over You

One of the most common arguments people use for becoming listless and rudderless when they have lost a partner or a child or a parent is that life has lost meaning because they are no longer here. And one of the most common phrases they use to sum this feeling up is: 'It's not the same without them being here to see it.'

People talk of their sadness at the fact that Grandad is missing out on seeing his grandchildren grow up. Or they mourn the fact that Dad is not around to see his son graduating from university. They get upset about the fact that a parent who has passed over isn't around to see his or her children opening their Christmas presents. The harsh truth is it is often an excuse for people giving up on life, for people failing to fulfil their potential or work hard to ensure their children fulfil all the possibilities within their life.

My answer to people who say these things is simple. To give up on something because you think a loved one is no longer here to see it is wrong. They can see it. They want to see it. We should do all in our power to help them see it.

The idea that loved ones who have passed over can see what is happening here on the earthly plane is a powerful one. People sometimes wonder how it works. Well, they see things through you.

As I have already explained, the journey is continuing for those who have passed over just as it is for us. We are both moving, in effect, along a set of parallel lines. We can't always quite meet, but whatever we are experiencing they are experiencing. We are running in unison with one another.

Sharing our experiences is a two-way street. If we are of a mind we can experience whatever they are experiencing as well. We can have that connection. It is something I will explore in more detail later, when I examine in depth the sort of signs and messages you will be able to receive when you understand the Message.

What's important now though is that we understand that while we can see and sense them they can also see and sense us. They can still watch what we are doing and they can interact with us as we do so. Which is why we have to carry on.

In this earthly life we are not humans having a spiritual experience, we are spirits having a human experience. And it's vital we remember that this physical life is full of opportunities and possibilities and adventures. The death of a loved one shouldn't be a reason to give up on all that possibility. The passing of someone who was important to us shouldn't mean we lose the opportunity to carry on with the human journey. Quite the opposite. It should make us even more determined to experience it to the absolute maximum. To live each day to the full. If we don't we bring to a standstill the whole process of the continuation of life.

This is why we absolutely have to carry on. All those experiences are passed on to our loved ones through us. And if we give up then we have deprived them of that chance to see their grandchildren grow up, watch proudly as their son graduates from university. By denying ourselves that experience we are also denying our loved ones the experience.

Let me share with you a story that illustrates what I am talking about here.

* * *

As I concentrated on the man who was coming through to me, as I performed at a large theatre in Surrey, I got a very strong sense that he was Polish by birth. I also sensed quite quickly that he was a serviceman, that he had fought for the Allies in the Second World War. I felt a connection to Italy, where I sensed he may have served. After the war he had come back to live in Britain and had been very proud of his adopted country.

He told me he was trying to get in touch with his granddaughter, Amy, who was in the audience. It took a while to find her, but eventually I did.

'I'm sensing a very *gentle* man,' I said. 'The sort of man who believed you must always go out into the world with a smile on your face. He never wanted people to see him unhappy, even when, towards the end of his life, he was finding it hard to keep smiling because of the physical pain he was suffering.'

'Yes, that was my grandad,' Amy replied.

His pride at having become a British citizen was obvious. 'After fighting with the British in the war he really felt this was his home,' I said.

'That's right,' she said.

'He never went back to the part of Poland he was from. It was a very poor place. He always said he belonged here, not there.'

'That's right,' his granddaughter confirmed

again.

As the connection grew stronger I got a very powerful sense of a self-taught man, someone who had read a lot and soaked up every bit of information around him. He showed me images of him endlessly reading newspapers and books.

'He is telling me that knowledge is empowering,' I said.

'Yes. He was self-educated,' Amy said.

As the connection continued I began to see that it was this subject, education, that had brought him through this evening. It was what he wanted to talk to his granddaughter about.

'He is saying that you must not give up on your learning. He is feeling that you are thinking of giving up,' I said.

Amy looked a little embarrassed at this.

'He is also showing me some certificates,' I said. 'He is saying that you must get the certificates out. Do you understand what that means?'

Her mother was sitting with her and she intervened at this point. She confirmed that Amy had some certificates that she never showed to anyone. She also told me that Amy had an ambition which her grandfather had known about when he was alive.

'She has always dreamed of being a teacher,' the mother told me.

'Your grandfather is saying that you must stick at it,' I told Amy, who was, by now, crying.

It was, I thought, a very poignant and very powerful message. Her grandfather had come from abject poverty in eastern Europe to make a good, respectable life for himself here. He had worked and studied hard to become a British citizen. He had valued education as one of the most important things in life.

Since his passing, Amy had begun to give up on life, and her studies in particular. Perhaps, somewhere inside her she had thought her grandfather was no longer around to see it. She was mistaken. He had seen it. And, as he demonstrated that night, he was determined to do something about it.

I have no doubt that Amy went home that night and dusted down her certificates, her sense of purpose in life renewed by her grandfather's message.

The Suitcase Under the Stairs

How are we going to realise our loved ones in our lives? What can we do to keep them close so that we know there is something of them there? A good way of answering these questions is to imagine that they are still with us in this life.

What would they be inspiring me to do with my life? Did they always encourage me in my career? If so then you have to keep pursuing that career. If they always inspired you in the arts or some other leisure pursuits, then keep that side of your life alive and moving forward.

You always have to take a long hard look at the nature of your relationship with the loved one who has passed over. Did they prevent you from achieving something or pursuing an interest? Perhaps you put aside something in your life because of the demands of your relationship with the person who has passed over?

If so, the way ahead may be to revive that

interest, to pick up again whatever it was that you put to one side.

A few years ago I gave a message to a lady from her mother. The daughter was middle-aged and had spent more than twenty years caring for her mother who had suffered a long and debilitating illness. She wanted to know that her mother was all right.

Her mother told her that she was fine. Her main concern was her daughter, who hadn't really seemed to move on with her life since her passing.

'Your mother is showing me a suitcase that is under the stairs,' I told the daughter. 'She says it contains some artists' materials.' The daughter smiled at this.

'Oh yes, I'd forgotten all about that old suitcase,' she said. She told me that she had been a very keen artist in her youth but when her mother had fallen ill, her time had become more and more taken up with caring. Even when she had had a spare hour or two to get out her sketchbook or easel, she was either too tired or pre-occupied with something relating to her mother. Artists need room to create. She didn't have any. Eventually she had given up and put the suitcase of paints and brushes away.

'Your mother is telling me that she wants you to get the suitcase out from under the stairs and to start drawing and painting again.'

It turned out that it had been the daughter rather than her mother who had made the decision to stop being creative. The mother had never been happy about it. She had always encouraged her to draw and paint and absolutely loved the work she produced.

'She is looking forward to seeing what you produce when you get that suitcase out,' I told her.

I don't know what happened to her but I would be very surprised if she didn't rediscover her love for her art after that. If she did, then I'm pretty sure she would have kept her mother's memory—and therefore her spirit too—very close indeed.

Something Old, Something New

A question I am often asked when talking to people who are moving on with their lives is this: if the person who has passed over can still experience what I am experiencing, how can I move on with another person? Many want to know: 'How can I experience life with them when my former partner is still around? Doesn't that make it difficult? Won't they be jealous?'

These are, to be fair, natural enough questions. But they are based on a false assumption, that the emotions we associate with this life are present in the next life. If the jealousies and petty rivalries that exist in this world also existed in the spirit world then it might be a problem. But they don't.

As I have explained already, the spirit world is a harmonious and peaceful place. All the jealousy and pettiness and possessiveness we can feel in this earthly existence is eliminated in death. Those who pass over transcend all those things. So those of us who are left living our lives here on the earthly plane must do the same thing. When it comes to the loved ones who have passed over, we must forget and transcend those things too. And that means transcending any ideas we might have about the person who has passed over being jealous of who we are now sharing our life with. As long as you are happy with that person they don't care. The person who you are sharing your life with now should know that too. They should not harbour any jealousies or guilt either.

This can, I know, be a tricky balancing act for people to pull off. If it does make us uncomfortable or we feel we need to do something tangible to clear the air, as it were, then there are some simple things we can do. We should already have got used to the idea of talking to those who have passed over. If necessary, we can do so again here.

For instance, this can be the point at which you thank the person who has passed over for the part they have played in your life and for having shared your earthly part of the journey this far. You can then go on to explain how you are going to continue that journey now with other people and new experiences.

You can say to them: 'I've got a new friend. They are not replacing you. They are different to you. I will probably go and do the sort of things I would have done with you but it will be different. I am continuing the adventure of life but I'm doing it with new people. I need to thank you for taking me so far in the journey.'

*　　　*　　　*

A few years ago I met a couple socially. They were really nice people, in late middle age. Stephen was a magistrate who I knew slightly. I knew that Janet was his second wife, his first wife having passed over a few years earlier. They were very interested in my work and we got chatting about some of my ideas.

I could sense where the conversation was going but that neither of them could quite summon the courage to ask me. Eventually, however, Stephen came out with it. 'I don't suppose you'd be willing to give us a reading, would you, Colin?' he asked, slightly nervously.

Naturally, I said I'd be delighted.

They were both a little nervous about what was going to happen. They sat there together, holding each other's hands tightly as I began. Their grip tightened a little further when I established a connection to a woman and began relaying a message from her. It quickly emerged that it was Stephen's first wife. I sensed that she had died of cancer.

'That's right,' Stephen nodded.

'She is telling me that you both cared for her while she was ill.'

'Yes,' he said, nodding again.

'She wants to thank you both for what you did.'

The mood in the room was quite tense now. I sensed that there was something that they both were waiting to hear from her.

'She is telling me how happy she is to see you,' I said. 'And she's saying that she wants you to know how pleased she is for both of you that you made the choice to be together. Despite what she said.'

At that point the couple both began shaking.

'She wants to tell you this,' I said. 'She says, "I would rather that you were with one another, than both of you were with someone else."'

The moment I said that, the pair of them burst into floods of tears.

When the connection faded, Stephen and Janet

told me more about what had happened a couple of years earlier. The two ladies had been best friends. When the lady who had come through to me had died Janet had felt the grief of her passing almost as acutely as Stephen did.

In sharing that grief they fell in love.

It is, of course, something that has happened before, and will happen again. Powerful emotions experienced in times of great change often bind us together, like this. But it was complicated in this instance by the conversations all three of them had during the lady's final weeks.

She had perhaps sensed how close her husband and her best friend were becoming as they cared for her. She had asked them both individually to promise her that they didn't get together after she passed over.

It is easy to cast judgment on someone for saying this. As I have explained, in this human existence we are prone to petty-mindedness, jealousy and selfishness. Let him cast the first stone.

So inevitably the pair of them had been guilt-ridden by their romance from the start. But their feelings for each other had been so strong they couldn't do anything but act upon them. They had married almost three years after the lady they both loved so dearly passed over.

Their life together had been happy. They had such a strong bond that they made a great couple—that was plain to see today. But the doubts over what they had done had lingered. They both still had huge issues over whether they had done the right thing. In the end they had decided to take the momentous step of seeking their friend's blessing from the other side.

It wasn't surprising that Stephen was a serving magistrate. He had an enormous sense of justice which, in this instance, had been eating away at him.

'We actually felt like we had betrayed her,' he said to me after the reading.

'We did the one thing we said we would never do,' Janet confessed.

I am often asked to seek approval for couples in this way. It is human nature for people, especially those who have been in long and happy relationships, to fret over whether they are doing the right thing in remarrying or settling into a new relationship. Especially when they have made promises in the emotional final days of their partners' lives. This illustration exemplifies something that we should all bear in mind when moving on with our lives having suffered a bereavement. We are often bound to promises that we should never have made. And those who have passed over to the other side often know this better than us.

*   *   *

I remember meeting a gentleman once who was in terrible turmoil about moving on with his life after his wife had passed over. A promise was at the heart of his dilemma too.

He and his wife were an extremely devoted couple and lived in a huge house on the south coast of England. They had spent years doing up the house and were particularly proud of the garden and orchard they'd nurtured there. They

154

both loved nothing more than sitting out in the grounds, listening to the sound of the sea in the distance. It was their little corner of heaven here on earth.

But then his wife had fallen seriously ill.

He had devoted himself to looking after her during her final days. Their house, and in particular their garden, had become a real source of solace to both of them. Towards the end of her illness, she asked him one day to make a promise to her.

'Please don't ever sell the house,' she'd said. 'I couldn't bear the idea of somebody else living here.'

Without really thinking about it, he'd agreed. Most of us would have.

He was devastated when his wife passed over but kept his bargain and remained in the house, rattling around in its huge rooms on his own and tending to their beloved garden and orchard. Time eventually took its toll, however.

Several years later, the husband, who hadn't remarried and had remained on his own, had grown old. He now found the physical strain of keeping the house and garden in the condition he—and his wife—expected a real burden.

The garden and the orchard had become a full-time job, one he wasn't physically equipped to do any longer. He couldn't hire gardeners to tend it. So he'd very, very reluctantly conceded defeat and started looking for a smaller place to live.

He'd found a small bungalow, not very far away. It was much easier to maintain and get around. It was near where his wife was buried too, making his visits to her grave easier. Everything about it seemed right. Except, of course, for the promise.

And so it was that he came to me for a reading. As I began, of course, I had no idea of the background to his story. I knew nothing about him at all in fact. So when his wife connected to me and began talking about this wonderful house, it meant very little to me.

She described some of the details of the house, the garden and orchard in particular. She showed me it was close to the sea. She told me how much she'd loved the place and how happy she'd been there, even during her dying days. It was clear the house had been a great solace to her during her illness, which pleased her husband.

The main message she wanted to get across, however, was that it was now time to let the house go. 'It has served its purpose,' were her precise words. 'You have got my permission to leave.'

The relief on her husband's face was immense. He was close to tears. It was exactly what he wanted to hear. As the reading came to an end, he explained to me how desperate he had become. 'I really didn't know what to do,' he said. 'I had promised her faithfully that I wouldn't sell it. I had done everything that I'd promised her I would do. But I'm too old now and it's just too big. To keep it on would have been impossible. I was trapped.'

I have come across many people who have been trapped by a promise in this way.

Invariably the message they receive releases them from the responsibility.

The Turning Point

A loved one's passing is an opportunity for you to

transform your life. What seems like a cataclysmic event can be the making of you. It can give you an incredible purpose and clarity in your life. I know this from personal experience. It happened to me.

In 1997 my closest and dearest friend, Michael, passed over. It was a shattering loss for me. But it was also a big turning point in my life, in fact *the* turning point. Michael's passing gave me a direction and sense of purpose that had, until then, been missing. It was at that moment that I decided to become a professional medium.

I have written about my Michael before but I make no apologies about doing so again. He was a family friend who became my closest friend. We seemed an odd couple in many ways. Michael was a former Barnardo's boy. He was twenty years older than me. When we met I was seventeen and he was thirty-seven. But from the beginning we were what I suppose you would call soul mates.

By the time I was in my mid thirties, in the 1990s, I had a very successful career in retail management. I made good money. I was, to a point, fulfilled in my job. At that point in my life mediumship was something I did at the weekends and during my spare evenings. Michael, however, believed that I should be doing more with this gift.

Michael was always the person who believed in me most in my life. My parents had been great supporters but they didn't have the kind of faith in me that Michael had. From the early days of our friendship he would say to me: 'There's something about you, something is going to happen to you.'

He had a gift for making me feel I was capable of conquering the world. And that's what he started encouraging me to do. With Michael

157

nudging me on I began to take my work as a medium further. Literally.

Slowly but surely I began to make an impact. I began to work more and more within the spiritualist movement. I took trips to Australia and Japan. I was extremely satisfied with the way things were going. I thought this is as big as it gets. I was still continuing my main career; I didn't think it was possible to commit myself full time to my mediumship. Michael, however, was determined to push me further.

We were talking one day and he got quite animated about the choice I now faced. 'What are you going to do?' he said. 'You are either going to remain successful in the retail industry where you're always going to make a good living. Or are you going to be brave and follow the other side of your life where you are making a difference to other people's lives?'

'Michael, I can't make a living out of it,' I said.

'If you are meant to you will,' he replied.

I wasn't brave enough to find out if he was right at that point. But then Michael got ill and everything changed.

In the mid-1990s he was diagnosed as being HIV positive. He faced up to his treatment stoically and with his usual good humour. Unfortunately, however, the therapy his doctors gave him damaged his cardiovascular system. In the end his heart gave out. He passed over in Kings College Hospital in November 1997.

Michael and I had come to regard each other as brothers. During his illness I became his next of kin, legally.

I had promised him I would be with him at the

end and I was. And the minute he took his last breath I took the decision. I am not going back to work; there are more important things to do in life. Michael's passing transformed my life.

Yes, I went through the process of grief like everyone else. I conducted Michael's funeral service myself. I dealt with all his affairs. I got power of attorney to deal with his estate after he passed.

But when all that was dealt with I basically took the plunge. I chucked in my job and walked away. It was, looking back on it, a crazy, rash thing to do. For a start, I had just taken on a new mortgage.

But from the beginning it just seemed to work out for the best. It seemed like the right thing to do. I supplemented my work as a medium with lecturing on positive thinking. Over the next five years or so, there always seemed to be just enough. Just enough to pay the bills, just enough to pay the mortgage. An unexpected bill would arrive and I would be asked to do a seminar. Then I was approached to do a television series.

When I was first offered a television series about my work as a medium, I turned it down because I was quite happy with what I was doing. I was working very successfully both in the UK and overseas. I had plenty of work and I didn't feel I needed the exposure that was going to come my way when I stuck my head above the parapet and appeared on television. Our work as mediums isn't always taken seriously and we're often ridiculed. Why would I want to invite that into my life?

The company were persistent, however. They kept coming back to me. And I kept saying no.

But then, slowly, over a period of four or five

159

days while these conversations were taking place, I noticed something peculiar. I kept seeing signs. A particular phrase kept jumping out at me. I saw it in newspapers, in books, heard it on the radio and on television. The phrase was 'out on a limb'. I'd read it for the umpteenth time when I finally gave in.

In the end I said: 'OK. I get it.' It was crystal clear. I had to push myself out on a limb, I had to leave my comfort zone and agree to do this television series.

Then a very close friend of mine also told me to do it. She said, 'You've gone through life thinking every opportunity you've been given is a gift. This is a gift. You are being given a chance to evolve and do more. If you don't do it you will be stupid.' I took her advice.

One hundred and thirty episodes of the *6ixth Sense*, and many other programmes later, I am still appearing regularly on television. My world hasn't fallen in. My life has changed beyond all recognition since.

I am convinced that none of that would have happened without Michael's passing. Often the changes that transform our lives happen slowly. At other times they hit us like a lightning bolt. That's what happened with Michael. The moment he passed over I remembered what he had said to me about the direction my life could take if I was brave enough to follow a different path.

I remember thinking vividly at the time 'there are more important things to do with my life'. It is now a message that I try to pass on to as many people as possible.

We all have the right to experience life to the

fullest. But instead tend to get bogged down in the details of life: how am I going to get the money for the tax bill, how am I going to afford to buy the kids new trousers when they go back to school, how am I going to deal with my relationship with my family, what will my friends think of me? We get weighed down with all this stuff. This new start in our life offers us the perfect opportunity to decide what life really is all about, to see whether there is a deeper more profound purpose to this earthly existence. We must all seize it.

PART SIX

Service

If spirits are being of service to each other on the other side then surely we should be of service in this life too.

Caring Spirits

During my three decades talking and listening, feeling and seeing the presences of those who have passed over to the spirit world, I have been given glimpses into what existence might be like on the other side. I believe the world that awaits us when we pass over is a very personal place. It reflects our individual beliefs about what 'heaven', for want of a better word, should be. The biblical phrase 'in my father's house there are many mansions' sums it up as well as any other.

But I am no more able to see into eternity than the next man. So I can't describe what it looks or feels like in any definitive way.

I have, however, come to know some things about the spirit world. One of the most important of them is that the afterlife is not a meaningless existence. By this I mean the other side isn't populated by millions and millions of spirits wandering aimlessly around. There is a purpose to what goes on there. There are such things as spirit guides and guardian angels, watching over souls on both sides.

The clearest evidence I have for this is the way in which the spirit world aids suicide victims. I get asked a great deal about people who commit suicide. What happens to those who take their own lives? Do they pass over into the spirit world in the same way as everyone else? Is their existence there as troubled as it was on the earthly plane?

There is a lot of tradition within religion that says people who commit suicide don't pass over as well as those who die a 'natural' death. According to the most extreme of these, of course, they are condemned to some kind of eternal damnation or hell.

During my thirty years as a practising medium I have relayed many messages from people who have committed suicide and I have come across no evidence to support this latter idea. However, I do believe that the act of suicide, and the huge emotional energy that has built up before it, does interfere with the energy victims carry with them as they pass over. It makes that transition more difficult. The period of adjustment that souls take to find their way and harmonise in the spirit world will be, inevitably, much longer.

That is the not-so-good news. The better news, however, is that once they have passed over, rather than being punished or placed in limbo, they are given extra help to regain their energy. It seems spirit guides help them in this, quite how I don't know.

I have thought for a long time that this is an extremely powerful truth. It confirms something that I have long believed, that giving something of ourselves to others is one of the most valuable things we can do. The only shame is that selflessness, sacrifice and service is in such short supply on this side of life.

I asked one of my spirit guides about this once and his answer was thought-provoking. 'You live in a world where people don't care enough,' he told me. I thought about it and it was so plainly true.

I remember that in a village near me in Sussex, a postman went eight days without noticing that somebody's post had been stuck in the letter box.

165

How has our society got to that parlous state?

How many of us check on our neighbours? How many of us worry about the single person who lives next door and who looks quite sad? Surely, it wouldn't take much to ask whether they are OK or whether they'd like a cup of tea?

I think the problem is, in part, to do with a false idea that many people have about what service really is. For some it is about being visible and being *seen* to be doing good work. It is actually self-serving, not selfless.

I was once told a story about a woman who went to see one of the great mediums, a man called Harry Edwards. She told him that she wanted to be of service to society. So Harry told her about a nursing home that was literally at the end of her street. It was a home for elderly people. 'Why don't you go there and offer one of the old ladies a cup of tea and a chat,' he said.

This clearly was not what this lady had in mind. She curled up her lip, wrinkled her nose and sneered: 'I don't mean that kind of service.'

Harry's reply to her was: 'Then you are no help at all.'

That lady's attitude typifies, I think, what is wrong.

The importance of service to others on the other side sends out a strong signal to me about the way we should be living our lives here on the earthly plane, nevertheless. If we are to stay in touch with those who have passed over we need to understand the principles that drive their dimension forward.

If it is at work on the other side then it should be at work here. So if we want to be in tune with the spirit world we should practise what they practise.

And that means that we should all strive to be of service.

Giving And Receiving

There is a quote I'm fond of by Albert Pine: 'What we do for ourselves dies with us. What we do for others and the world remains and is immortal.' Many people I meet believe in what are often called the fundamental spiritual laws. A lot of very gifted individuals use them in their teachings. These laws are nothing to do with religion. They are just basic spiritual laws.

One of these fundamental laws goes like this: the Universe, God or whatever you want to call it, will give us whatever it is we want in life provided we meet three criteria.

1. We know why we want it.
2. We know what we are going to do with it.
3. We know what we are going to put back for having received it.

It is one of the most important rules of existence, I think. It applies to the Message too.

Many of the people I meet in the course of my work know why they want to get a message from the afterlife. It isn't hard to work out. They want to be reassured that their loved ones are all right in their new existence. They want the peace of mind that comes from knowing that they have been able to connect to them.

Most people know too what they are going to do with the Message. Often it is going to give them the strength to do the things I have talked about

167

already, to commit themselves to a new purpose and direction in life, and to live that life to the full.

It is the third criterion that people overlook sometimes. And it is a question that you must address soon.

If you have followed the book this far, you are at a point where you may now be ready to receive a message of some kind, whether it is directly from the spirit of someone who has passed over, via a sign, or through a medium like me. As you prepare for this next, final step, you must ask yourself a question. If you are fortunate enough to be connected to the other side, if you do get a message from a spirit there, what are you going to do with it?

One of the most inspiring answers to this question was provided by a friend of mine from the spiritualist movement. His name is John.

John and his wife Geraldine were a very happy, generous couple who I'd initially met through the development circle I sat with each week in Sussex. It was in this circle that I really learned to understand and use my gift as a medium.

John and Geraldine had two sons, Howard and John. One day, when Howard was eighteen, he and his girlfriend were going up to London to see a show; so John and Geraldine gave him a lift to the local train station.

Being a good, caring dad, John told Howard and his girlfriend to sit at the front of the train so that they could get out quickly and avoid the rush when they reached London. The timings were a bit tight at the other end.

Howard and his girlfriend never made it as far as London, however.

The train was involved in a major rail accident in which a dozen or so people died. Those at the back emerged from the train virtually unscathed. Most of the casualties were at the front of the train, and Howard and his girlfriend were among them. They were both killed.

John and Geraldine were, of course, utterly shattered by the loss. It was hard enough to bear the death of their son in an accident anyway but to make matters even worse, John couldn't get over the fact that he had told his son to sit at the front of the train. He kept playing it over in his mind again and again.

In the months and years that followed, John and Geraldine's life went to pieces. John started drinking. Geraldine went into shock. She developed MS, something the family was convinced had been brought on by the shock of Howard's death.

They had both been stalwarts of the spiritualist movement in their area but they both lost their faith. This is common, of course. People of faith who suffer terrible losses often rail against God for letting it happen. 'Why didn't I get some warning?' John probably screamed at Him. 'Why didn't you tell me to put them on the back of the train?' Amid this sort of inner turmoil, many people can't forgive God for failing them and so they turn their back on religion. John and Geraldine's reaction was the same.

Now, standing back, I can see that they were making several mistakes. Most importantly they were tied up in the small picture. They were trapped by the circumstances of what had happened. They were failing to see the big picture.

Even though, of course, that big picture was something that was familiar to them as members of a medium circle. But, eventually, they did.

The way John told the story was that he was sitting up late one night. Geraldine had gone to bed. He became very emotional. And he just cried out: 'Howard, for God's sake, if you still exist, just give me a sign. Show me that it hasn't all come to an end.'

At that moment a fruit bowl that Howard had made as a boy at school lifted up off the sideboard and started floating across the room towards him.

Now some people might have their doubts about this happening but, knowing John and the kind of man he is, I have none. If he said it happened, it happened. I have no reason to disbelieve him. He told Geraldine about it and she believed him too.

It was the turning point. In that instant, John rediscovered his faith and his belief in the eternal life. He stopped drinking heavily and, with Geraldine, they started sitting in the circle again. Their faith had been restored.

Naturally, when they came back they were interested to get a communication from Howard. They wrote to the famous medium Leslie Flynn asking if they could attend a seance with him. To my mind Leslie Flynn was one of the finest mediums that ever lived. His book *Voices In The Dark* is one of the most inspirational I have ever read.

Howard came through in the reading. Leslie Flynn was a voice medium, able to convey the spirit's voice as well as its message, so John and Geraldine were able to hear Howard speaking to them from the other side.

He had some interesting things to say. He spoke about things that only Howard knew about.

Then he said something very strange. John and Geraldine have another son also called John. 'Tell John that I'm really pleased about the Brighton thing,' Howard said.

They all lived in London at that point. They had no idea what that meant.

'Which John?' his father asked.

'My brother John,' Howard said.

A couple of weeks later John and his young girlfriend said they were moving to Brighton.

Howard's mother and father continued to get communications from him within our circle too. At one of our meetings he came through and told them that they would be joining John and his girlfriend in Brighton. Again they were baffled by this. But then, through a strange and complicated set of circumstances I won't go into here, they totally unexpectedly found themselves buying a flat in Hove, adjacent to Brighton.

Slowly but surely, life started taking on meaning again. And for John and Geraldine that meant committing the rest of their lives to trying to help other people find this reality that life carries on. They also made a promise to each other that they would continue to do so when the time came for one of them to pass over.

The point of this story is that, a couple of years later, Geraldine had a stroke and died. Her funeral service was the most unbelievable and possibly strangest I've ever attended. The only people present at the crematorium were John, his son John and his wife with their two young children, me and the other members of the circle. There was no minister. There were no hymns or eulogies. We went into the crematorium where Geraldine's coffin was lying and some nice music was playing. We waited for the curtains to draw back and the coffin to slide out of view and then we all went back to John's house. There, we ate some sandwiches, had a drink and wished Geraldine well.

That happened on the Friday. On the Tuesday John was back in the circle. John's view was quite clear. 'My life will not end because Geraldine passed over,' he said to me. 'We absolutely believed in life after death and it would be an insult to her if I stopped going to the circle now. Especially after all we have been through.'

At the time of writing this, he is still going. He is quite elderly now, in his eighties, and a little deaf and disabled. To me he is the embodiment of the notion of service, of giving something back in return. Long may he continue to give back what he received.

Youthful Spirits

One of the reasons I still love my job, even after more than thirty years as a medium, is that it is never, ever dull. No two days are the same; no two readings are the same. It is always a journey of discovery. I am always learning something new. And I will continue to do so.

One of the areas that fascinates me most relates to children and what happens to them when they pass over. I am often asked questions about this. Do they continue to grow there? Can they connect? If so how do they communicate if they left this life at a very young age, before their brains developed fully. There are more questions than answers sometimes.

Some of the answers I am able to give stem from first-hand experiences that I have had.

A few years ago, for instance, I met a gentleman who wanted to get in contact with his son who had passed over. I arranged a private sitting with him.

I fairly quickly made a connection with a young man named Richard. The father was fairly certain that it was his son, although when I told him he was a beautiful-looking boy he looked unsure.

As more details came through, however, it was clear that this was his son, Richard. The messages he began passing on were warm and reassuring for his father. He said he was happy on the other side, which seemed to please his father particularly.

As the reading went on I began to get confused, however. 'I am seeing two people here,' I said to the father. 'There are two Richards. One is relating to this side and the other is relating to life on the spirit side.'

This didn't mean much to him so I continued, hoping things would clarify themselves. Eventually they did. I was soon seeing two distinct faces.

'One boy has the most beautiful face. That is the one on the spirit side,' I said. 'The other is, I think, a boy with Down's syndrome. He is on this side.'

'Richard was a Down's baby,' his father confirmed.

The impact of this reading on me was quite powerful. It was clear to me that Richard had been transformed on the other side. As I thought about it, it began to make some sort of sense to me.

In this earthly existence, the physical form is

often a limitation. It inhibits our growth and development. Freed from this physical imprisonment on the other side, however, we can develop differently. Richard's essential character was the same on both sides. What was different on the spirit side was that he was free from his illness and its debilitating effects. He was free to express the inner personality that had been hidden.

Interestingly it is akin to what happens with people who have been the victims of diseases of the brain like Alzheimer's. I have encountered many in readings and none show any signs of being mentally impaired on the spirit side. I think the same thing is at work there. Freed from physical confinement within their damaged brains the spirits are able to become their essential selves again.

In recent years I have also come to believe that when children pass over their consciousness becomes much more evolved than it was during their earthly existence. Again, it was a direct experience that led me to this.

A few years ago, I met a young couple who had lost their baby son in tragic circumstances. They had come along to take part in filming on one of the very earliest episodes of my television show, *6ixth Sense*. As the show began before a live audience, I had felt a very strong message coming through from a child who wanted to contact his parents.

I located this couple and invited them to sit on the sofa at the front of the studio with me. At first I found it difficult to identify the child. This, I discovered, was because I had never heard this name before.

'His name sounds like Marky or Mikey.'

'Yes. His name is Mika,' his parents said.

As I began talking to them all the details were correct. But what surprised me was the quality of the communication I was getting from the child. In particular, he wanted to thank his parents for the work they were doing to research the illness that had struck him down.

As well as providing me with an insight into what happens to children in the next life, their example also illustrated something else. They had been devastated by his loss. But they were able to move on, inspired by him. They set up a charity for young babies suffering from the illness that had claimed Mika's life. It had become a major success and was putting much-needed funds into the hands of research organisations all over the world.

This couple were, I believe, an example to us all. Many people feel that they are powerless to influence events outside their own life. They look at a situation in the world around them and say to themselves: 'I know what I'd do about that but there's no point in me trying. I am never going to change things.'

Well I don't believe anyone is too small to instigate change. Sometimes the most unlikely people make an impact on the world around them.

For an example of that, you only have to look back to the mid 1980s and the terrible famines in Ethiopia. Every night, millions of people watched the heartbreaking television images of what was going on there. The pictures of dying, starving and malnourished African children broke everyone's hearts. Most of the millions who watched were ready and willing to help but they felt powerless to

175

do so. They looked on and said, collectively, 'There's nothing I can do to help those poor children.' Even the world's governments were saying: 'Isn't it awful but there's nothing that we can do about it.'

It took an unkempt, foul-mouthed and unruly rock star to motivate the world into doing something. It took Bob Geldof to bang on the table and say: 'Yes, we can make a change.'

It was this spirit that drove on Mika's parents too. In the face of their loss, they had determined that their son's memory was going to live on through the work of their charity. Their selflessness was a reminder of the fact that nobody is too insignificant or too small that they can't go out and promote change.

PART SEVEN

Living the Message

When someone passes over, all that has gone is the mundane. The special moments can still happen, you've just got to be open to them.

Understanding the Essence

We should by now understand the essence of the Message. We should comprehend that life and death are two sides of the same coin. Heaven is not something far and distant. It is near and close. The life we live here on earth is only part of our journey. Our existence continues over there.

We should understand, too, that to keep the spirit world close to us we need to move on with our earthly lives. If we stop growing they move forward and we get left behind. They are evolving in the spirit world. We have to continue with the process of evolution in this life too if we are to keep in touch with them. We have to live the Message.

How we progress from here is a personal choice. We can use what we have learned to communicate through a medium. We can experience the wonder and wisdom of the signs the spirit world passes on to us. Or we can simply feel the closeness of our loved ones in a more personal way. It is entirely up to us.

So to close, let us look at the different aspects of the Message that we can now draw upon. In doing so we can see how others have learned to live the Message in a successful and meaningful way.

Live the Magic Moments

Many years ago I got to know a lovely woman who lived near me in Sussex. Her name was Mary.

Mary was a lady in her sixties who had been

widowed for twenty-five years. Her husband had died tragically young, in his thirties. She hadn't remarried but she wasn't in any way a sad or reclusive person. Quite the opposite in fact. Mary was full of vitality and life. She was always busy and I would often see her around interacting with her friends and family. What I found truly inspirational about her, however, was the way that she had maintained a relationship with her husband.

I visited her a few times and got to chatting with her. She quite openly told me that she lived her life as if her husband was still around. Mary would get on with her daily life just like everyone else. Then, just like everyone else, she would sit down in the evening and have a chat.

'I don't bother him with the boring things,' she told me once. 'It's only when something funny happens, or there's a piece of news that I think he'd want to know. Perhaps a birth or somebody else passing over from the village. It feels natural and there are times when I'm sure he's there listening.'

To me, there wasn't anything possessive or obsessive about this. I think there was one photo of her late husband in the house. She didn't talk about him incessantly in front of others, or mind if somebody else brought his name up. She did none of the things that I know can inhibit some people in moving on with their lives in a purposeful way.

She effectively treated him as any other wife in the area treated their husbands. The only difference in her case was that, while they spent most of their time in their potting sheds, on the golf course or down the pub, he spent all his time on the other side. Part of me wondered whether she might actually have had a better relationship than many of the ladies I knew!

I met Mary when I was still formulating the ideas that I have today. It took me many years to work these things out. She seemed to have understood them instinctively. Looking back I realise now that the simplicity of her thinking added enormously to my comprehension of the truth about our relationship with the afterlife.

The most valuable thing she taught me was that life is about the special moments we share. And those special moments are what can live on beyond this existence.

If we all sit down and think about it, this makes more and more sense. Our lives are largely made up of routine moments. In fact most people's daily experience of a relationship is pretty mundane. For most of us it involves getting up, eating, going to work, coming home again, eating supper then going to bed so as to start the same sequence all over again. It is all the usual, boring routine.

When you think about it, your happy memories are all made up of much briefer, unique moments. Whether it is your child's first footstep or a great dinner party, a special holiday or a wedding, a funny joke that will always remind you of something or being with someone watching your favourite football team winning the FA Cup or the Champions League. It's those magical moments that stay with you always.

Let me explain what I mean by sharing with you a memory of something that happened when I took three friends, Eden, Jane and Mark, for a walk one evening in Sweden, where I have another home. It was a beautiful evening and we had decided to walk up to a lovely lake in the hills nearby. The sun never sets completely in Sweden during the summer months, so throughout the walk we'd watched it dropping lower and lower in the sky.

As we reached the brow of the hill, overlooking the lake, it had dropped as low as it was going to go and it had cast this fabulous pink light right across the lake. The effect was truly spectacular. It was as if the sky and the sun and lake were merging into one.

We all stood there with tears running down our faces. My friend Mark was a big tough guy. He turned to me and said, 'This has got to be one of the most beautiful things I have ever seen.'

Now, if I'd seen it on my own, that moment would not have been anywhere near so special. Yes, I'd have appreciated the sunset. I may even have been moved to tears by it. But what made that moment truly special was that we were four friends together sharing this experience of this wonderful sunset.

Now it is safely enshrined in my memory as one of those magical moments in my life that I know I will never forget. And I know Eden, Jane and Mark won't forget it either. We experienced something fantastic together and that moment will bind us together always.

This is what I mean by special moments. They don't have to be momentous events. They can be the occasional look or touch, the odd funny experience shared with friends and loved ones. Those are the things that make relationships meaningful.

We all have to plod through the mundane. We all have to feed and clothe ourselves, get the kids off to school and pay the bills. This is the monotony of life. What makes our relationships with one another special are those, well, special moments.

When someone passes over, all that has gone is the mundane. The special moments can still happen, you've just got to be open to them.

You can't just sit there waiting for them to happen. You have got to get on with your life. And then they will happen just as they do in life, when you least expect them. Don't expect them to come with trumpeting choirs and a Hallelujah chorus either. They are much more subtle than that. They are much more like ordinary life here. If we understand the Message there is no reason why these magic moments can't continue.

Keep Them Near and Afar

As a practising medium I am very lucky. I can sense the spirits of those who have been close to me whenever I want. I have connected with everyone I know who has passed over. This hasn't always happened directly. On occasion I have had messages relayed to me through other people.

Six months after my friend Michael died, for instance, I received a very funny message from him.

Michael and I used to talk about death quite a bit before he passed over. A lot of people avoid the subject but I believe it's important we think about what is going to happen when we pass over. It helps those who remain here enormously in their grief, I believe.

For Michael and me it wasn't a depressing

conversation at all. For instance, during his illness Michael began losing his hair. He was bald by the end of his life and he used to joke with me that he would have long blond hair when he got to the other side.

Six months or so after he had passed over, I met another medium who told me he had been thinking of me a short time beforehand. 'I had this guy Michael with me,' he said. 'He wanted me to tell you that he's got long blond hair. Do you understand that?'

'Yes, I do,' I smiled.

I felt Michael around me quite often during that period. Now, more than a decade since his passing, I don't feel that connection as intensely as I once did because I don't need it any more. I don't need that confirmation. I know that he continues and I know that some part of him is often with me.

As we learn to live with the Message, this is an important point to grasp. We must neither expect nor want the spirits of our loved ones to be around all the time.

One of the most ridiculous things people say early on in their bereavement is how they miss having a loved one around 'all the time'. It's a phrase I hear often. 'My husband was with me all the time.' 'My mother never left my side.' 'I miss my daughter so much because I spent every second of the day with her.' I am always polite of course, but I have to tell these people they are talking complete nonsense.

Of course their husbands weren't with them all the time. If they were like every other husband that has lived, they spent a lot of time at work, in the garden, down the pub or playing golf. And of course their mothers weren't by their side constantly. Nor were their daughters with them all the time even when they were a baby. Sometimes they were put in a cot or a playpen so they could get on with their young lives. At other times they were sent off to playschool. It is simply unrealistic to think that someone is with another person all the time.

The reality is that we learn to live in the knowledge our loved ones are around. We don't need to feel them with us all the time. We don't need to see them constantly.

Take my mother and father, both of whom are still alive. They live just up the road from me. As I sit here and write this, I haven't seen my mum for about six weeks. But I don't need to. I don't need confirmation that she is still there. If she needs me she'll phone me. If she wants a chat she will phone me. And vice versa. I have my life to live. They have their life to live.

Exactly the same principle applies now that your loved one has passed over. You shouldn't desire the presence of those who have passed over any more than you wish for the presence of those who are here. Be realistic about this. Don't be over-sentimental about the person that's passed over. And don't say I want to be with them 'all the time'. That to me sounds more like hell than heaven.

Yes, you will have those moments when you will feel them. But don't expect to be talking to them or feeling them around you every moment of every day. Apart from anything else this is extremely selfish. They've got an existence to get on with. And so have you. Get on with it. Because, remember, if you don't you are the one who is breaking the connection.

Learn the Art of Communication

I've never felt separated from anyone who has passed over. At any time a thought, an experience or a memory will come up that makes me feel they are still connected with my life.

And I do feel the living force of their existence in my life. It isn't just associated to memory and wishful thinking that they are part of an experience I'm having at any particular time. I really do feel they are part of that experience. This is how I have come to think.

I know this is easy for me because of my gift. But my experience as a medium is only a more developed form of doing what I think anyone can do. For most people, communication with the other side may not be the same experience as it is for me. You may not feel the things I feel, sense or see the things that I sense and see. But you can have real experiences. And hugely positive ones too.

One of the most common criticisms of mediums is that we bind people into their grief, that we prolong their anguish. I have never tried to bind anyone into their grief. Quite the opposite, in fact. I've always tried to free people from their grief.

I believe by understanding the Message I have tried to explain in this book, you can free yourself. Once you've acknowledged their existence continues and connects to yours, you can move on. But you have to acknowledge that they have moved on as well.

In a sense, you are just being asked to learn

185

another life skill. Another communication skill, to be exact. It is one that involves learning to keep a relationship alive when the physical presence is gone.

It is something to be celebrated. It is a joyous thing. What is really great about it is that all the mundane things that bogged you down are gone now. There is no more going to work, no more going through the chores of life. You are now completely free to have special moments.

It should be a joy. Everything that is going to happen now is going to be about the special moments that make human relationships worthwhile. The human experience is all about the pursuit of the occasional special moment. It is the same when we look at our relationship with the spirit world.

Earlier on in this book I compared our separation from those in the spirit world with having a friend or family member emigrate to a faraway country. I think this is a good analogy, in many ways. It can help us all understand how, over time, we can develop a relationship with a person who has passed over. For the sake of argument, let's imagine someone is emigrating from the UK to live in Australia. But let's imagine they are doing so two hundred years ago. The only way they are going to be able to communicate with people back in the UK is by letter. That letter is going to have to travel by boat and will take several months at least to get to its destination. It will then be another few months before they can expect a reply to find its way back to them in Australia. Was it any wonder that when people emigrated abroad then it was like a bereavement?

So any communications we receive will be special. Our loved ones are going to take a lot of time and trouble to convey as much as possible about what has been going on in their lives, especially as those letters are only going to be sent four or five times a year, apart from birthdays and Christmas.

I talked earlier about the tiny percentage of the person that remains in contact when they physically move to the other side of the world. This form of communication was the ten or twenty per cent that they could hold on to. Now, of course, communication is much easier. International telephone calls are cheap and we have emails and webcams. But in fact it hasn't changed the physical disconnection. Realistically it is still only that small percentage of the connection that is there.

So this is still a good way of thinking about how we are going to connect with those who have passed over.

*   *   *

At this point, of course, you may well be thinking about going to a medium to help you make the connection you are seeking. If you have followed what I have explained in this book so far, then I would say that your chances of having the person come through to you are probably reasonably good. Especially if you remember all I said about being positive and open in your demeanour and body language.

But, whether you go down this route or any other route, you will probably find that, to begin with, communication is not going to feel easy. At

187

first, it is going to feel like relying on long distance letters back in the nineteenth century. The more you continue to live the Message, the more you move on with your life while holding their memory near and close, however, the easier the flow of communication will become.

If you visit a medium repeatedly, you may find others coming through to you. To refer back to the Australian analogy, at first it will be like the occasional phone call. But when you get to that state of mind where you acknowledge an existence beyond this one you will begin to feel more connected. They will never be online all the time of course!

The other thing that will happen is that your conversations or connections will become more meaningful. Again, it is like the progression you would see as you communicated regularly with someone on this side. The more you get to know someone, the easier the conversation flows, the less inhibited the two parties become. And so it will go on.

The more you embrace the Message the easier it will be. It's not just about learning how to have a conversation. It's about developing the art of conversation as well.

Often in messages there are references to past events or memories and then the spirit makes an observation about what that connection is continuing to do in life. If, for instance, you were to get a communication from your uncle George who taught you to love fishing when you were young he might say something like: 'I was with you the other day when you went fishing. Do you remember when we went fishing?'

If you stop the continuation of experience, there is nothing more to talk about. This is why, once again, it is so important to lead a life that is full of meaning and purpose. The more you have done in your daily life, the more news you will have to catch up on if you do make a connection.

In the same way, if you fall back into some of the other bad habits we looked at earlier in the book—possessiveness, obsessiveness, etc—then that too will have the effect of drying up the conversation. Be sure to avoid them too.

Honour the Things They Stood For

By honouring the principles and beliefs of those who have passed over, we make it possible to keep a really strong and powerful connection alive. It isn't always easy to do this, of course, especially when it requires the co-operation of others. Nowhere does this apply more, of course, than where family are involved.

The important thing, however, is to persevere. The rewards will justify the effort. It will draw you closer to the spirit you are honouring with your actions.

The example of a lady I met while on tour in New Zealand illustrates this rather well. Cindy was in the audience when I received a connection from Doreen, who turned out to be her mother.

From the beginning, it was clear to me Doreen was a plain-speaking woman. I had to edit her for public consumption as she complained about several things. First she moaned about the opera music her daughter was playing in the house when she did her cleaning. 'It puts me off visiting you,' she told me. She also said that she wasn't happy that they had only fitted 'twelve crappy words' on the memorial plaque the family had constructed for her.

But she had a more serious message to deliver. For generations, it seems, there had been simmering tensions in this family. 'It's as if they are constantly at war,' she told me. Since her passing things had gone from bad to worse, culminating in a confrontation between two brothers.

'She is giving me the feeling that an almighty argument had kicked off. One brother tried to attack the other brother with a knife,' I said.

Cindy nodded to confirm this.

'Would you understand that if we go back a few generations there were always members who were at each other,' I said.

Cindy nodded again.

'Your mother is showing me that things have changed drastically in the past seven months. But it took you blowing your top to sort it out,' I said.

At this point she began crying.

'You didn't like saying anything because you liked to keep the peace. But it ended up blowing out of all proportion,' I told her. 'Your mother is telling me, "I know that feeling, love, because that's what I did until I had to do exactly the same as you and blow my top."

'Your mother is telling me that she is proud of you for stepping in and breaking them up. She says you really had to blow your top with them,' I said. ' "Just like I had to do." '

Cindy smiled and nodded. 'Yes, I did,' she said.

It was clear that there were still tensions in the family. Doreen asked her daughter to sort out her relationship with her sister too, which she promised she would. But there was no question that her mother had come through to tell Cindy how proud she was of the work she'd done in bringing some sense of peace to her warring family.

'Your mother is thanking you for all the effort you have made to make sure everyone gets along now,' I said. 'It's what she would have done had she been there. But she is glad that you have stepped into her role.'

Talking to Cindy afterwards, she revealed how dramatic her intervention had been. She had found her two sons confronting each other ready to inflict serious harm. She had stepped in at great risk to herself. 'I don't believe in fighting. I put myself between them,' she explained.

One of her sons made as if to hit her. As he did so she screamed at him. 'I said, "If you are going to hit me make it a good one,"' she confided. Her actions had taken the steam out of the moment. Seeing their mother blow her top like that had also knocked some sense into her sons. She admitted there were still rifts in the family but they were getting better.

The fact that she'd got the message from her mother moved her deeply. Cindy felt sure it was going to help her heal the remaining wounds within her family that much more easily. Given the way she was living the Message, I had a strong feeling that was going to happen sooner rather than later.

Never Forget

The links between the spirit world and this earthly life are open at all times. If you are of a mind, you can feel the presence of those who inhabit this other dimension at any time too, not just when you are in the presence of a medium.

It's important to know that the spirits watching over you aren't all your immediate friends and family. Sometimes your interests are being guarded by other, equally well-meaning influences. If you keep them in your heart and in your mind, then they too can connect with your life in a meaningful way.

One evening, as I began describing a primary schoolteacher who had worked in the 1960s or 1970s, a middle-aged man made himself known in the large theatre audience.

The moment he did so, I experienced a very warm feeling towards him from the spirit communicating through me. The name I'd been seeing was a Miss or Mrs Jackman or Jackson.

'Yes, Mrs Jackson. She taught me at primary school,' confirmed the man, who identified himself as Neil.

'Neil, she's telling me that she liked you,' I said. 'You were allowed extra milk.'

The man smiled and nodded at this. He did so again when I described how Mrs Jackson was showing me that he had a mild speech impediment when he was at primary school.

'Yes, that's right,' he said. He also confirmed, to his mild embarrassment, that Mrs Jackson was right too, in that he used to have a crush on a girl called Penny. 'That's correct too,' he blushed.

I sensed that Mrs Jackson had a more serious reason for coming through, however. 'She wants to let you know that she knows that the year leading up to the spring of this year was one of the most difficult of your life.'

He nodded.

'She just wants you to know that you have not been alone. She is saying: "Even though I have been unseen and unheard by you, I have been there to nudge you in the right direction."'

'Yes,' he said.

Mrs Jackson went on to show me a very serious situation that had developed at Neil's workplace. He seemed to have been involved in some kind of dispute with his boss, one of the directors of the firm he worked for.

'Sometimes directors are idiots and they don't recognise talent when they see it,' I said. 'She is showing me that you have made some difficult decisions. But you did not at any point lose your dignity.'

As the reading went on I saw that the bad management decisions that Neil had argued against had cost the company £20,000. 'That's correct,' he said. 'If they'd listened to me they'd be £20,000 better off.'

The reading cheered him up enormously. It turned out that Mrs Jackson had been a strong influence in Neil's life. In life, as in death, she had become something of a guardian angel.

Neil's speech impediment was, in fact, part of a more serious condition. He had Asperger's syndrome, a form of autism. It was a condition that was little understood at the time. Despite this Mrs Jackson had instinctively helped him out.

'Mrs Jackson gave me extra one-to-one lessons. She was a bit of a hippy but she wasn't soft in any way,' he said. 'She would praise you when you did something right. But she would not let me become lazy or lose focus.'

Neil sensed that she understood his Asperger's before it was diagnosed many years later, when his son was found to have the condition as well. 'Looking back, she would have been a great special needs teacher. She seemed to understand my problems in a way that nobody else in school ever did,' he said.

Mrs Jackson had been killed in a motorcycle accident with her husband in the 1970s. But Neil had continued to think of her. During the thirty or so years since her passing, he had felt her presence a few times before this evening.

'It's funny, I am aware of her being around when things are difficult,' he explained.

This was clearly why she had come through tonight. Neil confirmed that he had been in a long-running argument with his employers, an engineering firm. He sensed that he might be about to lose his job. The problems had been going on for the last year. There had been an argument over a piece of engineering equipment. His company director had refused to accept Neil's expertise in the matter and ignored him. It had cost the company in excess of £20,000.

The dispute and the stress it had caused had taken its toll on Neil. As Mrs Jackson had seen, the last twelve months had indeed been the most difficult of his life. He had sensed Mrs Jackson's presence at the height of his problems. 'I felt her about a year ago,' he said. 'I had been feeling very negative. Just like at school she had come along and told me not to give up.'

He was overjoyed at feeling her presence again through me. Once more she gave him the strength to carry on as he prepared for another difficult period in his life.

Neil was made redundant a week after my reading with him. But just as Mrs Jackson had taught him, he refused to give up or get downhearted. Soon afterwards he began a legal action against his firm. As he prepared for a long court battle, I felt pretty confident that his guardian angel was going to be watching over him every step of the way.

See the Signs

As I mentioned earlier in this book, when I was sixteen I had the honour of meeting the great English medium Doris Stokes. A friend of mine knew her and invited me to meet her backstage after her show in Brighton. It was a huge thrill for me, a moment I have never forgotten.

Doris Stokes was a much derided figure in some circles. But she was hugely popular and very much loved by her many thousands of fans. She was also a wonderfully warm human being. What few people know is that she gave virtually all her money away. When she died she left only £20,000 or so, a small fraction of the fortune she made from her performances and bestselling books. The rest had all been given to charities connected with children, the cause to which she gave a great deal of her life.

The debt of gratitude the modern generation of mediums like myself, Derek Acorah and T.J. Higgs owe Doris is immense. I think it's fair to say that we would never have had the opportunities we have had if she had not paved the way.

Today I travel the world performing. As I do so I also get to meet other mediums. Among them is my American colleague, John Edward, someone I admire enormously.

Recently, while John was in London to perform at the Hammersmith Apollo, we had lunch together. It was a rather pleasant, convivial affair. Over a glass or two of wine we chatted about all sorts of things, not just our work as mediums.

At one point, for no particular reason I began talking about my grandfather, Lawrie. As I have already explained, he was a hugely influential person in my life, someone who has remained close to my heart throughout my young and adult years. As I did so I kept referring to the way he called me 'Sonny Boy' all the time. It didn't really register at the time, but as I did so John kept smiling at me warmly. I guess I thought he was touched by the affectionate way I spoke about my grandfather.

It was only during his show that night at the Hammersmith Apollo that it became clear why he was smiling actually.

During the show, John very graciously pointed me out in the audience. I stood up and accepted the applause.

John had been talking about the importance of the signs that we can sometimes be given by those who have passed over into the spirit world. He was explaining how they are around us at all times. 'For instance, Colin inadvertently gave me a sign today at lunch,' he said.

He went on to explain that an uncle, Sonny, had passed away shortly before he had left the United States. He had been very fond of him and he had been upset at the loss. On the transatlantic flight, John explained that he had asked for a sign from Sonny while he was in England.

'While we were having lunch Colin kept talking about how his grandad used to call him Sonny Boy,' he explained. 'And at that moment I knew this was my uncle Sonny's way of sending me a sign.'

*   *   *

You have reached a really exciting point. Once you open up your mind to the idea that there is not this huge barrier between the two worlds a whole new way of seeing things begins to present itself. Understanding that those who have passed over to the other side remain close to us opens up all sorts of possibilities.

As I have said, you may choose now to start seeing a medium or to attend spiritualist gatherings. But you can also independently begin to see the signs of the eternal life that exist all around us.

I passionately believe that there are signs linking us to those who have passed over. They are present in the most ordinary and mundane details of daily life. You only have to be of a mind to see them.

They can be the smallest things, perhaps a song that unexpectedly comes on the radio, or the sight of something long forgotten that reminds you of

197

them. It might be contained in something that someone, unwittingly, says to you. Just as it was for John Edward one day when I had lunch with him.

Whatever it is, however, it can connect you to the person who has passed over in a powerful, meaningful and often truly beautiful way.

The great thing about signs is that they are there for everyone to see. You don't have to go to a medium to see them. They are all around us, all the time, provided we are of a mind to see them, as I did when I saw the sign that told me to 'go out on a limb' and become a full-time medium.

And once you've developed this attitude of moving on without forgetting those who have passed over you will start to feel those moments when something of them is there. A thought, a memory, something you see or hear or do will draw them straight back to you. And when that happens you won't need a medium to confirm it to you. You will know it was a sign.

Recently, for instance, I was walking around the aisles of a local supermarket. I was browsing in an area of the store that I would not normally have visited. As I scoured the shelves, my eyes settled on something that I hadn't seen in years.

It was a tin of condensed milk. Actually, it wasn't any old condensed milk, it was a particular brand: Fussell's. I just stood there smiling because it reminded me of my paternal grandfather. Although we weren't always that close, he had moments when he could be incredibly funny. And one of the things which never failed to amuse me about him was the way he used to open a tin of Fussell's condensed milk and just sit there and eat it with a spoon.

I'm sure one or two people in the supermarket must have thought I was slightly deranged for standing there looking at this tin of milk and giggling away to myself. But I didn't care. In that moment everything that I remembered about him came back to me.

Even though we clashed quite a lot, I learned a great deal from him. He was a man with very different ideas to mine, so much of it was to do with what I didn't want to be rather than what I did want to be in life.

In time, though, you do reach that point where you remember the good things about people that you didn't acknowledge in life. And as I stood there nursing this tin of condensed milk, I spent a moment or two remembering the good times I'd shared with my grandfather.

This had nothing to do with my mediumship. It was simply that I had been open to receiving a sign. Signs occur when the bridge between them and us becomes very narrow and you can still feel them close to you in your life. They can be very light moments, like the one with the tin of milk, or they can be more serious.

One evening, for instance, I received another sign that proved to be incredibly timely. It may even have saved my life.

I was heading home from Brighton where I'd been meeting someone. The drive back into the Sussex countryside is one I make all the time. I always follow the same route, through Ditchling. This evening, however, as I reached the junction that would have led me up to Ditchling Beacon and Ditchling village as usual, I saw a black cat run across the road in front of me.

Now I am not in any way superstitious. So the fact that a cat had passed in front of me had no significance in that sense. What it did do, however, was remind me of a friend.

This particular friend always took the appearance of a black cat as a sign that he should change his route. If he saw one he would take the next junction or even turn around and head in another direction until he found his way home. He simply regarded it as a sure sign that there was trouble further down the road he was heading.

The night was closing in and I was keen to get home. But the sight of the cat and the memory of my friend triggered a thought in my mind. I thought this is telling me not to take my normal route. I need to turn off here and go another way.

It was back home that evening while watching the evening news that I heard about the horrendous pile-up that had happened on Ditchling Common an hour or so earlier. It had been a terrible crash and there had been fatalities. Ambulances had been brought in from all over Sussex and the roads had been closed off, resulting in traffic chaos in the surrounding area.

There is no doubt I would have been in the area at the time. Given the timing of the accident, there was a really high probability that I would have been involved.

Every now and again I hear a story of someone who has had a similar experience and seen a sign that has made an important different to them. They always make me smile.

Often a sign appears because someone is actively looking for some signal of approval, a hint that someone on the other side approves of what is happening in this earthly existence. This is what happened to a lady called Rosalind, who I met when I was doing some charity work a year or two ago.

Rosalind's daughter had died of a rare, genetic illness a year or two before I met her. The loss had, of course, been traumatic for her but it was made even more painful by the circumstances.

Rosalind had taken the decision to keep her daughter in the dark about the real extent of her illness. This was a big step. The advice the family were getting from the doctors was that the girl should be told. They felt it was more ethical and would, in the long term, help her cope with her situation better.

Rosalind, however, disagreed violently and she had stuck to her guns, despite the pressure from family members and doctors who kept insisting that she should tell her daughter the truth.

They had their opinion. Rosalind, on the other hand, genuinely believed it was helping her daughter to live a relatively happy life for as long as possible. She still believed that when she died.

She had had regrets about what had happened, of course. During her bereavement they had eaten away at her along with her grief, making it a long-drawn-out and painful recovery process.

Eventually, however, Rosalind emerged and as is often the case, she channelled her grief into charity work. In her case, however, it seemed a highly appropriate step. The charity was raising money for research into the genetic disorder that claimed her daughter's life.

As Rosalind began working with the charity, her expertise was soon being called upon. One day she took a call from another mother whose daughter was dying of the disease. She was on the horns of the same dilemma as Rosalind had faced. She couldn't decide whether to tell her daughter about her illness.

Rosalind still passionately believed she had made the right choice and advised the mother to do the same, to withhold the truth from her child.

Rosalind was not a reckless person, far from it. She was a compassionate and caring woman, with a strong sense of right and wrong. Despite this, however, she once again worried deeply about whether she had done the right thing. She knew that it was an individual decision and everybody was going to have a different attitude.

As she worried about this she kept thinking: *I want a sign, I want a sign that I've done the right thing.* She quickly saw one.

When her daughter had died, Rosalind and her family had planted a rosebush in her memory. Oddly, however, the flowers had never bloomed in the right colour.

That year, however, a single rose did bloom in the right colour. She saw it as a sign that her daughter approved of what she had done.

Waiting For God

There is a very good joke about a man who was waiting for God to appear to him. He had been caught in a flood and was marooned on the roof of his house. He had asked God to save him.

As the waters rose, a boat suddenly appeared. 'Hop on board, son—you're saved,' shouted the man steering it.

202

But the man on the roof waved him away. 'No thanks. I'm waiting for God,' he said.

The boat travelled on and soon the waters had risen even further. Suddenly a helicopter appeared, hovering above the house with a rope ladder lowered from it.

'Quick, grab this,' shouted a voice from inside the helicopter. 'We can fly you to safety.'

But again the man stood there shaking his head, refusing to accept their help. 'No, I'm waiting for God,' he said.

The helicopter had others to rescue so didn't hang around.

Soon afterwards the waters consumed the house and the man was drowned.

When he got to Heaven and found God waiting for him he protested: 'Where were you? I was waiting for a sign.'

God just shook his head and looked at him. 'What do you think the helicopter and the boat were?'

*   *   *

In life we are always looking for the obvious. And we are always expecting too much. The signs are always all around us. We just need to be of a mind to see them.

See What You See

People often say to me, 'Do you believe in fairies, or angels?' I say I believe in elemental forces which can sometimes manifest themselves here on the earthly plane. But if you are asking me do I believe in little winged creatures that prance around the garden then probably not.

It is all about perception, how you see things. I remember once having a conversation with some students. As I walked into the room I discovered them having a very heated conversation about whether angels had wings. They asked my opinion. 'What do you think, Colin?'

I began by asking one of the male students to describe what a fairy looked like.

He looked at me as if that was a stupid question. 'Wings, part human, like a butterfly,' he replied.

'Are you sure?' I said. 'Did you know that the modern concept of fairies comes from Victorian fantasy writing. If you go further back into fairytale literature, fairies were often described as tall, blonde wood spirits. Our image of fairies is a Victorian invention.' I went on to explain that the same thing applies to angels. 'The angelic form was an artistic impression created by Renaissance painters. If you look at angelic forms going back they were earthbound figures. They looked more saintly and had halos. There were no wings.'

The point about this is that when we encounter signs of a life beyond this earthly one, what we see is a matter of what our minds can accept. It is, I think, related in some mysterious way to what happens in the afterlife. There the environment we experience is dictated by our consciousness. We see what we want to see. It is the same here on the earthly plane.

So as a result of this, all signs are, by their very nature, intensely personal things. People will see what they want to see.

I am often asked, for instance, about people

204

who claim to have seen the Virgin Mary. 'No one else could see it, so why should we believe that they saw it?' they wonder.

My answer to this is simple: it was real to them. What you perceive as a sign will be meaningless to somebody else. And so it should be. If it is a sign it is a sign to you. And you alone. No one else should be able to see it.

Signs are very liberating. If your mind is open to it, you can interpret things pretty much any way you want to interpret them. I always get annoyed with fellow spiritualists who push this idea of guardian angels or guides, telling people they have to believe in them. Nobody has to believe anything. Yet, having said that, if that's what *you* want to believe then that's fine. So if you experience a sign and you want to regard it as the action of someone in particular, a guardian angel, you can think that way. If, on the other hand, you can't acknowledge or comprehend that concept, that's fine too. Not everybody has to sign up to that way of thinking.

We can still be open to signs without accepting that there is some great angelic force looking over us. We don't even have to call them signs. We can call them coincidences, if we want.

Not long ago, for example, I bumped into a lady that I know in a coffee shop near my home. As we waited for our coffees we started chatting.

'Colin,' she said to me, slightly apprehensively. I could see she was bit self-conscious. 'There's something that's been bothering me. I have this robin that always comes and sits on my windowsill at the same time every day.'

'OK,' I said, intrigued.

'The thing is it comes at 12.45 p.m. the exact

time when my husband passed over. Every day. I think it's a sign that he is still around.'

Now there are many ways you could interpret this. A sceptic would ask her whether she perhaps puts food outside at this time of the day. It might be that the robin has got used to this and habitually turns up on the off chance.

On the other hand, some people might have taken it to the extreme and said that the robin was actually her husband, returning to see her. Personally, I don't toe the reincarnation line and I certainly don't toe the line that we reincarnate into an animal. But it is a belief system. If that's the basket people want to put their eggs into that's fine. But she wasn't interested in either of these explanations.

To her the robin's appearance every lunchtime was simply a small sign that something of her husband was still in existence. And it was showing itself to her, at that significant time every day. Whether or not this was true didn't really matter to her. It was a great comfort to her. So she chose to believe it. I believe she was quite right to do so.

Not all signs are so ephemeral, however. Not all are open to question or to personal interpretation. Sometimes they are just blatantly obvious.

As you move forward you may well become aware of obvious signs too. Say an old friend phones you up out of the blue asking you to do something which you associate with the person who has passed over. Perhaps up until now you hadn't associated this friend with the one who is no longer here? Is that a sign that you should accept the invitation? Probably.

You see an advert in the newspaper for a job

that you'd always said you would like to do. Is that a sign that you need to move on? If you believe it is time to move on, then yes it is.

Signs are, as I say, entirely personal. Sometimes, however, they are irresistible too. The ability to see and understand signs is all about being in the right state of mind. If you are of a mind to see them, they are everywhere. If you are not, you will not see them—even when they are literally in front of your face.

One of the most powerful and inspiring books I've read in recent years was called *Signals*. It is the story of two American friends, both of whom contracted HIV. The two men weren't lovers, they were just incredibly close. Sadly one of the two died, leaving the other distraught. As he continued to struggle with his illness, he desperately missed his friend. Every day he longed for a sign that he was still there, but saw nothing. He was desperately looking for something. But he couldn't see it.

As time went by, his condition deteriorated further. His treatment wasn't going well and he began to give up hope. He thought it wasn't worth carrying on. There is no point, he told himself.

So he decided he was going to end it all. He got everything prepared, bottles of pills, alcohol, razor blades. He decided he was going to take all the pills, drink all the alcohol, get in a hot steaming bath and cut his wrists.

On the evening he decided he was going to kill himself he began running the bath. It was the middle of winter but for some reason he had a top window open in his flat. Just as he was preparing himself for this act of suicide, a hummingbird flew in through the gap in the window.

It was freezing cold outside and was totally the wrong time of year for a bird like that to be around. But it was there.

The bird didn't flit around the room in a panic as most birds would. Instead it arced around and flew towards this guy. It then stopped right in front of his face and just hovered there, as if talking to him.

Finally, the penny dropped. When his friend was alive the pair of them had had a fascination with hummingbirds. Since his friend had passed over, he kept seeing them wherever he went. He saw their distinctive features on mugs, posters, in magazines, everywhere. He would walk into shops and there would be carvings of hummingbirds. It got to the point where he couldn't go anywhere without seeing one. Yet he had thought nothing of it.

As he sat there watching this one, however, there was no escaping the inevitable conclusion. 'If this isn't a sign then I don't know what is,' he said to himself.

The moment transformed his life. It shook him out of his self-pity and forced him to re-evaluate everything. More than anything, however, it made him realise his closeness to the spirit side and the possibilities that opened up to him.

He went on to write his book, pass on his message and inspire many thousands more people to look for the signs that surround us all the time.

Be Patient

Some of the most common questions I'm asked about communication with the spirit world are about time. 'How long will I have to wait for a message?' 'My mum's been passed over for ten years now. Why hasn't she come through?'

I am always honest with them. I suggest that maybe they don't see any purpose or reason to come through. Perhaps, as I have explained already, they themselves are not sending out the body language that says they are open to a message. Perhaps they haven't come to terms with themselves or the person who has passed. Perhaps they haven't reconnected to the world and moved on with their life.

But mostly I give them a simpler answer: 'Well, maybe they're just not ready yet.'

Since I began practising as a medium thirty years ago, everyone I have ever known in my life has connected with me from the other side, either directly or through another medium.

The quickest this has happened was within forty-five minutes of the person's passing. At the other end of the scale, I have had personal experiences while communicating with spirits where the person making contact passed over seventy years earlier. So, as you will see, it can vary enormously. I have given up trying to work out why this is.

One thing I do know is that it takes longer for some to make the transition into the spirit world. It is not always an easy process. I have had communications from spirits who have told me that the transition is hard work. As one of them rather colourfully put it to me: 'Dying is bleeding tiring!'

They need a period of adjustment. There is a very good reason for this. I believe that death is traumatic in the same way that birth is traumatic.

We are moving into an environment that is alien to us.

A child in the womb might be able to sense what is going on outside. We know the foetus is sensitive to light and sound and chemical changes within the mother's body. But ultimately the unborn child doesn't really know what lies in wait in the outside world until it goes through that trauma of birth. The more I interact with spirits who have passed over to the other side, the more I believe that it must be the same for people at the end of this, their earthly existence.

One of the things that come up in messages is that although there is no physical dimension to the other side, it still requires a period of adjustment for them to recover their energy. This seems to be the case particularly if they have been through a long-drawn-out death or been in an accident or a violent death. It can take longer for them to adjust to the other side.

My point here is that we have to be realistic about making a connection with the other side. More importantly, we must be realistic about what we expect of the person who is passing over. They are going to need a period of adjustment when they arrive on the other side. For some it is going to take longer than others. The key thing is to be patient.

Believe What You See

For me the paranormal is normal. I have been receiving messages since I was a child. I consider it part of my everyday life.

For most people, however, it is an unusual,

210

remarkable and unbelievable event. It need not be this way if you understand, believe in and live by the Message.

One evening a lady at a theatre in London described to me a vivid dream she had had in which she communicated with her mother on the other side. I could see as she recounted the memory that it was a happy experience. Her face was wreathed in a big, beaming smile.

'Is it true Colin?' she asked me. 'Did it really happen?'

Well, the first thing to say was, yes, it is possible she did have such a dream. The spirits of our loved ones can connect with us in three different ways. They can appear in a manifestation, in which we physically see them. These, I have to say, are rare. Or, of course, the second way they can communicate with us is through mediums. But they can also appear to us in dreams. These can be very vivid, very powerful communications.

A lot of people come to me in the way that this lady did. They can't quite believe it. This is, sadly, because those around them are telling them it can't be true. Society shakes its head and says it can't be so.

I often say that truth is a double-edged sword. One person's truth is not another person's truth. Some people will say: 'I believe you' while others will not. In the end, however, it doesn't matter what anyone says. No one can take away the personal experience that you have felt. Your truth is what happens to you. And that is the truth you must listen to and hang on to.

This is what I told this lady: 'My darling, the saddest thing would be if you dismissed your communication because friends, family or society in general says it didn't happen even though you know it did,' I said.

You must listen to your own truth. And you must believe in it.

Tap into the Power of Places

As I have said, the gap between the two worlds can be as thin as a hair or as wide as an ocean.

If we want to feel close to the other side we must do what we can to keep that gap as narrow as possible. Only by doing so will we be able to bridge the divide.

One of the most obvious and effective ways we can feel and make a connection with those who have passed over is to revisit places that were important to us when we were together on this side. The shared memory brings us closer. The power of place acts like a magnet, drawing us together.

Persuading people to do this, however, can be difficult. Many of us simply don't want to revisit places that, we assume, will stir up nothing but bad memories.

As I explained earlier, I would always encourage people to revisit familiar places early on in the days after a bereavement. By creating new associations we can reshape our view of the world in which we are now living. But for some people this is simply too much.

Over the years I have spoken to many, many people who steadfastly refuse to visit places that played an important part in their lives when their loved ones were with them. They will refuse to go to a favourite restaurant, bar or pub ever again because of the feelings it stirs up within them. They will go to great lengths to avoid a favourite walk in their park. They will shun holiday spots that hold strong memories of happy times in the past. They always say the same thing. It is too painful. It will bring back sad memories.

The irony of this is that at the same time, these are the very people who tell me that they are looking for a message, that they want to feel close to their loved ones who have passed over.

My response to these people is always the same. If you are avoiding those favourite places, how on earth are you going to feel close to them?

The importance of all this was brought home to me one night when I was performing at a large theatre in the city of Hamilton in New Zealand.

As I began describing the woman who was trying to communicate with me, I didn't mince my words. 'In life this lady was quite harsh,' I said. 'But I can sense she had a wry, crooked smile as she said things.'

The connection was being directed towards a middle-aged lady sitting near the stage. She confirmed she was the daughter of the lady coming through.

'I get the feeling you could never be sure if she liked you or not because she came across as being so harsh,' I said to the lady.

She nodded.

'Do tell her I'm actually beginning to quite like her now. Not only do I quite like her now but I need her to know I always did love her,' I said.

At this the lady began crying.

'It was always a battle of will and wits between

you and her,' I said.

'That's true,' she agreed.

'She's showing me that it's sad that it is only now she is on this side that you can really understand one another.'

As the reading continued, however, the mother told me about a moment she and her daughter had shared many years back. It was clearly an important memory for her. 'She's taking me back a very long time to when you were nine or ten. She is saying: "You will remember, dear, we had one truly happy day at a park. We had one day where all the differences between us began to evaporate. That's how you should remember me."'

It was a very emotional reading.

The daughter admitted that life with her mother had been very difficult. She had been one of five children and she had felt like a slave when she had been growing up. It sounded like her mother had made her life a living hell. As a result, their relationship had been a difficult and distant one. They had not been close and had remained cool towards each other, even towards the end of her mother's life.

I have passed on many communications in which those who have passed over say things that they were, somehow, unable to say when they were living their earthly existence. This is the transforming effect of the afterlife. All that was suppressed and held in within the body and mind in this earthly life is liberated on the other side. We all find peace and harmony there.

In this case, the mother was now free to express the emotions that she had felt too constrained and, perhaps, fearful to express when she was here.

They boiled down to that one simple phrase that means so much to us all. She just wanted to tell her daughter that she always really did love her.

'She was the last person in heaven I expected to come through,' the daughter smiled afterwards. 'To hear her say that finally was wonderful.'

What stuck in my memory about this particular reading, however, was a smaller, seemingly insignificant little detail. It was hidden in the mother's memory of their one, perfect day together, that 'one truly happy day at a park'.

The message was a significant moment for the daughter who had clearly been struggling to come to terms with her mother's passing. She and her mother were both now ready to move on with their very different existences, but to do so with a closeness they hadn't experienced perhaps even in this life.

What struck me as being rather beautiful about the message, however, was the fact that it had showed the lady exactly how to keep that closeness alive. She could do so in that park.

'That's how you should remember me,' her mother had said.

The lady didn't mention her mother's memory of the day in the park afterwards. But as she dwelled on the message in the days and weeks that followed, I hope she realised that she had been given a wonderful gift, a clue about how she could now keep her mother's love as close as she wanted.

I don't know whether the daughter had been walking in that park often since her mother's passing. I got a sense that she hadn't. Perhaps, like so many people, she had been avoiding it for fear of the mixed emotions and memories it provoked.

I really don't know where it is, or indeed if it still exists. But wherever it was, it now provided that lady with a link to the afterlife. It had taken her mother's message to lead her there.

I believe we can all draw on the power of familiar places in this way. Rather than avoid them for fear of the negative feelings they may evoke, we should embrace them. They bring us closer to those with whom we once shared them. They are the places where the gap between the earthly and spirit dimensions is always going to be as thin as a hair.

Follow Their Guiding Lights

I believe that the spirits of those who have passed over are always around to help us. We can all gain solace, comfort, guidance and support from them. They can be the guiding lights we need in difficult times.

During the course of my work I frequently see them pass on priceless advice to those who are struggling to cope with life here on the earthly plane. To the audiences that witness them they may sometimes seem small and insignificant messages. But often they can provide beacons of hope. When it comes down to it, they are the most compelling testimonies to the power of the Message.

Let me share with you two brief stories that illustrate what I mean.

The man coming through to me was a real character. He was as thin as a rake, wearing a baggy vest and had bits of tissue paper on his face after cutting himself shaving.

216

In the background I could hear Cilla Black's big hit record from the 1960s, 'Alfie'. 'What's it all about, Alfie?' she was singing.

'I feel his granddaughter is very important to him. She was much younger when he passed over,' I said.

A lady in the upper circle of the theatre made herself known.

'That sounds like my grandad. And my son's called Alfie,' she said.

I was getting a very strong message from her grandfather that she had not been allowed to see him during the final days of his life. 'I feel like you either couldn't see him or were prevented from seeing him when he was ill because you were so little,' I said. 'It was because he was in such a poor and sickly state. Your parents told you that you would not have wanted to see him at the end.'

'Yes,' she confirmed.

'He is trying to show me that you were allowed to wave to him through a window before he got really ill. You had to be lifted up so you could see through.'

'Yes, that was the last time I saw him,' she said.

The man was very happy to see his granddaughter, who was now in her mid thirties, I'd say. But he was also very keen to talk about this boy called Alfie. This was why the line, 'What's it all about, Alfie' kept playing in my head, I realised.

I kept seeing this boy jumping around like Batman and Superman. My head was filled with images of him leaping off furniture all over the house. I saw that, if it hadn't been for his great-grandfather, this might have been his undoing.

'He is telling me that Alfie almost pulled over a

217

wardrobe,' I said. 'He is saying: "I'm there trying to hold it up as he's trying to pull it over."'

It was then that he got to the important part of the message he wanted to get through. 'He is saying you were right to hold back on some medical treatment for Alfie,' I said. 'You were right to say "let's see what happens". Your grandad is saying you should not get too upset about the medical treatment. You are making the best decisions you can as a parent.'

Afterwards the lady revealed that her son Alfie was autistic. He was a very active boy and could be a real handful at times. He had indeed pulled a wardrobe down on top of him once. 'That was one hundred per cent right,' the boy's father confirmed.

Alfie's condition was obviously a great cause for concern and his parents had been seeing various doctors. Like any good parents in this situation, they had been agonising over the right course of action. Their grandad's words of comfort had been just what they wanted to hear.

'The great thing was knowing that the decision we are making about our son is one hundred per cent right. We made the right decision to hold back,' Alfie's mother said.

*   *   *

As we have seen, those who dwell in the afterlife have a strong sense of service, sometimes a stronger sense than we have here in this life. They are ready and waiting to guide us when the going gets tough, as a young designer called Nicky discovered when she got a message from her grandmother.

218

Nicky had recognised it was her gran when I had begun talking about an incident involving cooking a curry.

'This lady thought she knew better than everybody else when it came to cookery,' I said. 'She is showing me an incident when she ruined someone's curry.'

'Yes, that's my grandmother,' Nicky said. 'She was quite a scary lady.'

Vera had come through for a specific reason, I felt. Nicky was a very attractive young girl. But her grandmother was worried that she was not making the most of her looks. 'Your grandmother is fed up with you not appreciating that you are a beautiful girl,' I told Nicky.

But she was also concerned that she wasn't doing enough with her life in the wake of her passing. I got the strong sense that this lady was a domineering influence in this life. From the other side, however, she could see that she needed to give her granddaughter her freedom.

'She would not have had the same attitude when she was in life, but now she is saying you have to get your own space. You must be whatever you want to be,' I said.

In particular, she felt Nicky wasn't fulfilling herself professionally.

She had seen a design Nicky had been working on. 'You have done a design in purple and silver,' I said.

'Oh, my God! Yes, I did it today,' Nicky replied, slightly shocked.

'Gran is saying, "Don't you dare give up on it. It's the best piece of work you've done. Don't give up on it."'

In life I believe we all have a choice. We can be the product of what happens to us. We can be the product of what others do to us. Or we can be the product of what we do for ourselves and what happens as a result of that.

The spirits of our loved ones know this. Sometimes they need to remind us.

Believe in the Message

Not everyone who comes to my live shows is absolutely convinced that what I do is genuine. Some of these people turn up because they are plain curious. They have, perhaps, watched me on the television and been intrigued by what they've seen. They have come along to see what the fuss is all about. They aren't quite sure what to make of it. I welcome these people with open arms, always. It's a matter of pride to me that, quite often, they leave the theatre having had their minds changed.

Every now and again, however, I am confronted by outright sceptics, people who think communicating with the spirit world is nonsense, all smoke and mirrors. After thirty years doing what I do, I don't need to convince anyone of the validity of my work. And, having survived three decades of ridicule and snide comments from certain quarters, I gave up worrying about what other people think about my work a long, long time ago. To be honest, I have never understood why these people come along in the first place. I don't like football so I don't go to football matches. If you don't believe in mediumship, then why waste perfectly good money on coming to one of my psychic medium shows. It makes no sense.

The reason I have very little patience with these people, however, is the fact that, by coming to one of my shows, they dishonour the memories of those loved ones most of my audience are carrying with them. They also disrespect those people who have come along in the genuine hope of receiving a message. Those who believe in the work I do.

Those who don't believe will, one day, discover the truth. Of that I have no doubt. For those who do believe, however, it is important that they keep the faith. Living the Message is about believing the Message. We must believe in its power. And we must keep our faith in that belief.

*   *   *

Time and again in my shows, I see the benefits that belief brings with it.

One evening, for instance, while performing to an audience in the Midlands I was aware of the presence in my head of some rather nice jazz and blues music. It was connected to a man who was trying to come through to two women in the audience. Spirits don't always speak to me directly. Often all I get is a jumble of feelings, images and thoughts out of which I have to make some sense. This is what I was working with in this case.

I got a very strong sense that this man had passed over having had cancer. I also sensed that two or three members of his family were in the theatre this evening. When I said this, a blonde lady towards the back of the hall put her hand up and identified herself as this man's daughter.

'He is giving me the feeling that he knew he was not well a long time before he told you,' I said. 'He kept it from all of you because he felt he was doing the right thing in doing so.'

'Yes,' his daughter replied.

Almost immediately, however, he indicated to me that he wanted to speak to the lady sitting quietly next to his daughter.

As the microphone was passed to her he spoke a simple sentence through me. As he did so I could see he was wearing the biggest, broadest, most charming smile.

' "See, I told you I would find a way to come and say hello," ' I said. It was clear that this meant a great deal to the lady. She was his wife.

The man was keen to tell her how happy he was on the other side. 'He can now sit and listen to his music uninterrupted, without anyone saying "can you put something else on",' I told her. 'He always liked it quite loud. He is sitting there with this jazz and blues music blaring away.'

As it turned out, the daughter had come along with an open mind. Her mother, however, had arrived in the theatre believing. It was her birthday and her belief had brought her a rather lovely present.

It wasn't the most dramatic message I have ever delivered. But it did sum up something very important. If you believe, then somehow, some day they will find a way to get through to you. We have to keep the faith to give the time to do so.

A similar thing happened at another show, this time in Kent. The lady in the audience seemed reluctant to acknowledge the fact that the couple I was describing sounded exactly like her parents.

The message was coming from a man who had a wonderful relationship with his wife. They were a real, what I like to call, 'Darby and Joan' couple. They used to tease and be rude to each other mercilessly. He used to call her an old bag and she called him an old git. But heaven help anyone who was rude to either of them. 'Don't you dare talk to my other half like that,' the other would say.

The more I communicated about her mum and dad the more vigorously the lady nodded her head. Her face was a mixture of laughter and tears.

During the connection I had a clear image of a lady belting someone over the head with a shoe. 'She's a real character, your mum,' I said.

She nodded her head again.

I also saw them sitting in a pub where there were lots of horse brasses on the wall.

'Dad drank in a pub called the Running Horses,' she confirmed.

I said, 'They were the sort of couple who would go to the pub, sit there in silence for a few hours, watching everyone else, then go home telling each other, "That was a good night."'

I had a clear vision of her sitting at home reading her *Woman's Weekly* and him constantly fiddling with the watch he was convinced was broken.

'That's right,' she smiled.

'And I can see that she never let anyone get past the kitchen unless she knew them really well.'

'No, she didn't.'

It was clear to me that neither could live without the other and that their lives on this side came to an end within a short time of each other.

But from the effort he was making to communicate with me, it was also obvious that the man had made a huge effort to make the connection tonight. I explained, 'He is telling me that he once said: "I don't know what happens when you die but I will try to get a message to you no matter how long it takes."'

At this she was nodding her head.

His final words to her were simple but heart-rending. 'I'm sorry that it has taken me this long,' he said.

Share the Message

As I explained at the very beginning of this book, some people have an instinctive understanding of the relationship between our world and the other side of existence. They know that the spirit side is close and that we can keep our loved ones close too. They are, in a very real sense, living the Message.

Often this understanding is something that has been passed down through a family. It is shared knowledge that trickles down through the generations. This can be the source of enormous strength when those families go through difficult times. So it proved when I united four members of a family in New Zealand.

The first person to come through to me was a young girl. She gave me the impression of being a very sweet child. She seemed to be trying to connect to her mother.

It was, however, her aunt who was in the audience. It turned out she was one of two aunts from this family who had come along to my show that night.

The little girl, Louisa, had quite a lot of things she wanted to get across. One message was to her father. '"Daddy did not really do a bad thing and

I'm happy that it was realised," ' I told the aunt.

She nodded.

I knew I had to be sensitive about the details. 'She is telling me Daddy had been accused of doing something but someone had lied about it,' was all I said.

The little girl seemed more worried about her mother, however. 'Mummy has got to stop making herself sick,' she told me. 'Do you understand that?' I asked.

'Yes, I understand her grief,' the aunt said.

'I think it goes a little bit further than that, my love,' I said. 'The little girl is telling me she has got to stop making herself sick because she can't come to me yet.'

She also mentioned a child who was on this side. 'There's a little girl who sees her and talks to her and talks about her,' I said. The other aunt in the audience nodded.

At this point I was also joined by a gentleman who had a very strong association with both aunts. This turned out to be their grandfather.

His arrival prompted the little girl to reiterate her message to the mother. 'You are both going to have to be united in getting through to your sister. She has got to pull herself together and she has got to get her will to live again because it is not doing your niece on the spirit side any good at all,' I said.

'Thank you. She's given us that message before,' one of the aunts said.

The most important remaining message came from the grandfather.

'Be reassured that he is looking after her,' I said. 'The only thing he objected to was the inappropriate use of the words "rest in peace" being used somewhere. In a memorial or service somewhere. He says she doesn't rest in peace. She lives in peace.'

Afterwards the two ladies confirmed that their niece had died a few years earlier. She had been seven and a half years old when she had died instantly in a car accident. Her mother had been driving.

They knew that their sister had been fighting a battle to remain strong in the wake of the tragedy. 'Our sister has always been a very strong lady throughout all this and been determined that friends and family see her as being strong. Inside we know she is going through a lot,' they said. But their niece's message had alerted them to the fact that she may not be succeeding.

The family was clearly comfortable with the idea of the spirit world connecting and communicating with us here in our life. The little girl who was mentioned in the message was one of the ladies' daughters.

'From a very young age she had felt that Louisa had been to see her,' I said.

It was clear too that the grandfather had felt the loss as keenly as anyone. But he had been a key figure too in keeping alive the family's faith in the eternal nature of life.

'He always used to say, "If they were going to take someone it should have been me." He used to say, "She lives in peace, she lives amongst us and we mustn't forget that,"' one of the sisters said. 'And he always said, "I will look after her when I'm up there."'

So it had proved. The image of the two generations of the same family sharing their existence together in the spirit world must have been enormously comforting to the two sisters. I hoped it was going to be even more so for their sister, as she still struggled with her grief over her daughter's death.

I had no doubt that this family would continue to communicate with each other across the dimensions. I felt sure that—thanks to experiences like the one they had shared that night—they would continue to pass the Message on down the future generations. The Message was always going to live on in them.

Never Forget That . . .

- Grief is not something that has to be endured for the rest of your life.
- Tears should be saved for joy and memories.
- We should look to the future not the past.
- We should not waste emotions by turning time into something negative.
- We must avoid negative statements and expressions.
- Negative thoughts will only lead to negative outcomes.
- We must be realistic in our expectations.
- We must not romanticise the person that's passed over.
- We must not desire the presence of those who have passed over more than the presence of those who are here.
- Some people never change. Try not to be one of them.

The Middle Ground

If you look at the history of spiritualism, the reason it really took off during the Victorian period in particular was that the established religions weren't giving people the answers they wanted. It was still the time when within a family of three children at least one child was expected to die. There were great advances of science which were providing a lot of answers. But people wanted something that occupied that middle ground between faith and science. And spiritualism for many people was that middle ground. And I still think it is.

Spiritual thinking occupies that middle ground between the decay of religion and the fact that science is too clinical and final when it deals with death. Any scientist can tell you about the physical facts of death but they can't tell you anything about what happens to the mind when the body decays. They will say that it is human arrogance and ego to believe that something of us continues.

If that was the case why is there a history going back to the dawn of time where people have sensed and even seen that there is more. Since I was a child I have been able to see, hear, feel and sense there is more. I don't think that is something that should be dismissed so easily. Particularly when I see it doing so much good. Particularly when it gives people a belief that can bring them moments like those I have described throughout this book.

I'm not being a medium all the time. Yes, I am aware of the spirit world always. It's there constantly. But I don't usually connect to it unless I'm working. If I was to connect into it constantly, if I were able to provide an endless stream of connections, which thank God, I'm not, I'm sure people would have no appreciation of its value.

To me the important thing is that we live life by adding to our own experiences on this earthly plane and really appreciate those moments when we get special connections.

The greatest thing I could imagine would be if, in one hundred years' time, people like me were no longer necessary. We mediums only exist because people do not accept the continuation of life. Once we, as a human race, have evolved to a point where we have accepted that existence, people like me will not be necessary any longer.

If you've read and understood this book then we have taken one step closer to that day. Until it arrives, however, I will remain around to do my bit to help people experience those special moments.

A Moment on a Mountain

The people who deal with grief and the loss of a loved one most successfully are the ones who make significant life changes.

They deal with the initial shock and grief and from there they start progressing forward asking themselves the fundamental questions we must all ask. 'How do I live my life from now on?'

'How do I live my life in a way that not only honours that person but means that I'm doing something that has purpose and meaning?'

These people are very often the ones who are rewarded with the truly special moments that keep the connection with the other side alive.

I was fortunate enough to meet, a few years

back, a lady who epitomised this approach to life after bereavement. Her name was Jennifer.

Jennifer had been happily married to her husband Jim for more than thirty years. They were both in their early sixties and were heading quietly and contentedly towards retirement. As couples do, they had even started planning what they were going to do at that stage in their life. Travel was top of their list. They weren't sure whether they were still up to it, but they were determined to try anyway. They had a dream of backpacking around South America, and the Andes in particular.

As the old saying goes, life is what happens when you tell God your plans. With no warning whatsoever Jim fell ill and was diagnosed as having terminal cancer. He faded fast. The cancer overcame his body very quickly. In the space of a few, dreadful months, Jennifer saw her husband succumb to the ravages of his disease. She was, of course, bereft at his loss.

It took her a while to re-adjust. But, in time, she emerged to start her life anew. As she did so, Jennifer made some big decisions immediately. The one thing she was not going to do was sit around and mourn Jim's passing for the rest of her life. She missed him dreadfully, but she knew he wouldn't have wanted her to sit at home crying. She also sensed that, somewhere, he was moving ahead with his existence. She had to do the same thing.

So Jennifer decided to take drastic action. She wasn't going to be able to go backpacking in South America with Jim. But she could still go on her own.

So, in her mid sixties, she completely changed

her life. She sold the big old house that she had shared with Jim and scaled down to a much smaller flat. She then used the money she had spare and took a huge chunk of their life savings and headed off on a massive, year-long trip around the world.

High on Jim and Jennifer's list of places they really wanted to visit was the amazing, mountaintop city of Machu Picchu, high in the Peruvian Andes. Set in the clouds at an altitude of around 8,000 feet, the stone settlement was once home to the Inca civilisation.

Jennifer had been determined that she was going to make it to Machu Picchu. She was three quarters of the way up on the climb to Machu Picchu when she had this incredibly profound experience.

She was standing there looking out over the lush, green mountains, their peaks disappearing into the cotton wool clouds. It was an awe-inspiring sight.

All of a sudden, Jim was in her head talking to her. 'This is everything we ever dreamed we were going to do,' he said.

She hadn't even been thinking about him. She had been drinking in the beauty of the scenery. But he was there, his voice as clear as if he were standing next to her.

There were no tears. No feelings of regret or sadness that Jim wasn't physically there to share the moment. Instead Jennifer stood there with this broad grin on her face. It was the highlight of her holiday.

It was after she returned from Peru that I met her. She'd been so overwhelmed by the power of that simple little moment high in the Andes that when her year-long adventure was over and she returned to England, she began to take a keen interest in mediums. She came to see me perform and I met her at a reception beforehand.

It wasn't that she was looking for more messages from Jim. She knew now that he was safe and well on the other side. She spoke to him regularly around the house when she had news to pass on.

'I've had that experience that shows me life does go on,' she told me. 'I am now just interested in seeing how mediums convey that to people.'

What a great example of how I try to tell people to live their lives after bereavement, I remember thinking when I heard her story. You can't just sit there waiting for those magic moments to happen. You have got to get on with your life. And then they will happen just as they do in life, when you least expect them. Just as it did for Jennifer in the Andes.

EPILOGUE

The Weeping Willow

I began this book with my grandad Lawrie, the person who first introduced me to the truth about our existence. It was he who showed me that there is an eternal life and that it is a lot closer to this earthly life than most people know. It was he who gave me the Message that, I hope, you will now be able to embrace and apply to your own lives. So I think it is only fitting that I end with him too.

As I explained, he was a powerful presence when I was in my teens. During the first few years after his passing, I frequently felt, heard and saw him guiding me on my way. His presence, although less frequent than back then, has remained with me ever since. I still have special moments when I experience him, sometimes in surprising ways.

Not very long ago, for instance, I was in my garden in the Sussex countryside. It was a lovely spring day and I'd decided to tidy things up after the long winter. I love pottering in the garden, but I have to confess I'm not very good at it, mainly because I don't know what I'm doing. I don't know the difference between weeds and flowers. Give me a trowel and I will dig up a perfectly good flower because I think it's a weed. I can look at something and think to myself, 'Oh yes, that needs pruning or cutting back.' But then I will hack it back to death because I have no idea what I'm doing. That was what I was doing on this day.

My partner Mikey and I had only recently moved to this property. One of the reasons we bought it was its garden, a lovely, rambling space with a pond, flowerbeds, shrubbery and trees. On this particular day, Mikey and I were looking at a tree at the bottom of the garden.

'That's a nice weeping willow,' Mikey said.

Without knowing it I suddenly found myself saying: 'No, that's not a weeping willow, that's a weeping silver birch.'

'How did you know that?' Mikey wondered, slightly taken aback at my sudden transformation into Alan Titchmarsh.

For a split second I had to think about it myself. I don't think I'd ever consciously known there was such a thing as a weeping silver birch before. But as I analysed my thoughts I realised what had happened.

'My grandad just told me,' I said, smiling.

My grandad Lawrie had, unlike me, been a great gardener. He'd spent endless hours with a hoe or a spade in his hand. If he was not down on his knees planting something he was in the potting shed at the bottom of his garden. He was a great reader as well and knew the names of seemingly every plant, shrub and tree that had ever taken root.

As I'd stood there looking at this tree, I'd heard his voice in my head, telling me it was a weeping silver birch. For a few moments I was aware of a flood of information in my head. If I'd been asked to name any plant or tree in the garden at that moment, I would have been able to do it, I'm sure.

The moment passed in an instant. I was soon restored to my normal, enthusiastic amateur gardener self.

It is now many years since my grandfather passed the Message on to me. Ever since, I have worked to spread that Message. Death is not the close of a relationship. It is merely the beginning of a change in the nature of that relationship. You can still have those special moments of closeness and communication. Whether it is something tangible or something more ethereal doesn't matter. They don't have to be qualified or justified or explained. They are your experiences. This is what living the Message is all about. My grandfather had reminded me of this again in the garden that morning.

If you keep them in your heart and in your mind, if you move on with your life in a way that honours their memory and adds meaning and purpose to what remains of your earthly existence, then you too can experience those special moments.

So keep the faith. Believe in the Message. And some day, some way, they will find a way of reaching you.